I0170499

DICTIONARY
THEME-BASED

British English Collection

ENGLISH-ALBANIAN

The most useful words
To expand your lexicon and sharpen
your language skills

3000 words

Theme-based dictionary British English-Albanian - 3000 words

By Andrey Taranov

T&P Books vocabularies are intended for helping you learn, memorize and review foreign words. The dictionary is divided into themes, covering all major spheres of everyday activities, business, science, culture, etc.

The process of learning words using T&P Books' theme-based dictionaries gives you the following advantages:

- Correctly grouped source information predetermines success at subsequent stages of word memorization
- Availability of words derived from the same root allowing memorization of word units (rather than separate words)
- Small units of words facilitate the process of establishing associative links needed for consolidation of vocabulary
- Level of language knowledge can be estimated by the number of learned words

T&P Books Publishing
www.tpbooks.com

This book is also available in E-book formats.
Please visit www.tpbooks.com or the major online bookstores.

ALBANIAN THEME-BASED DICTIONARY
British English collection

T&P Books vocabularies are intended to help you learn, memorize, and review foreign words. The vocabulary contains over 3000 commonly used words arranged thematically.

- Vocabulary contains the most commonly used words
- Recommended as an addition to any language course
- Meets the needs of beginners and advanced learners of foreign languages
- Convenient for daily use, revision sessions, and self-testing activities
- Allows you to assess your vocabulary

Special features of the vocabulary

- Words are organized according to their meaning, not alphabetically
- Words are presented in three columns to facilitate the reviewing and self-testing processes
- Words in groups are divided into small blocks to facilitate the learning process
- The vocabulary offers a convenient and simple transcription of each foreign word

The vocabulary has 101 topics including:

Basic Concepts, Numbers, Colors, Months, Seasons, Units of Measurement, Clothing & Accessories, Food & Nutrition, Restaurant, Family Members, Relatives, Character, Feelings, Emotions, Diseases, City, Town, Sightseeing, Shopping, Money, House, Home, Office, Working in the Office, Import & Export, Marketing, Job Search, Sports, Education, Computer, Internet, Tools, Nature, Countries, Nationalities and more ...

TABLE OF CONTENTS

PRONUNCIATION GUIDE

T&P phonetic alphabet	Albanian example	English example
[a]	flas [flas]	shorter than in 'ask'
[e], [ɛ]	melodi [mɛlodí]	absent, pet
[ə]	kërkoj [kərkój]	driver, teacher
[i]	pikë [píkə]	shorter than in 'feet'
[o]	motor [motór]	pod, John
[u]	fuqi [fucí]	book
[y]	myshk [myʃk]	fuel, tuna
[b]	brakë [brákə]	baby, book
[c]	oqean [ocɛán]	Irish - ceist
[d]	adoptoj [adoptój]	day, doctor
[dz]	lexoj [lɛdzój]	beads, kids
[dʒ]	xham [dʒam]	joke, general
[ð]	dhomë [ðómə]	weather, together
[f]	i fortë [i fórtə]	face, food
[g]	bullgari [buɬgarí]	game, gold
[h]	jaht [jáht]	home, have
[j]	hyrje [hýrjɛ]	yes, New York
[ɟ]	zgjedh [zɟɛð]	geese
[k]	korik [korík]	clock, kiss
[l]	lëviz [ləvíz]	lace, people
[ɬ]	shkallë [ʃkáɬə]	feel
[m]	medalje [mɛdáljɛ]	magic, milk
[n]	klan [klan]	name, normal
[ɲ]	spanjoll [spaɲóɬ]	canyon, new
[ŋ]	trung [truŋ]	ring
[p]	polici [politsí]	pencil, private
[r]	i erët [i érət]	rice, radio
[ɾ]	groshë [grófə]	Spanish - pero
[s]	spital [spitál]	city, boss
[ʃ]	shes [ʃɛs]	machine, shark
[t]	tapet [tapét]	tourist, trip
[ts]	batica [batítsa]	cats, tsetse fly
[tʃ]	kaçube [katʃúbɛ]	church, French
[v]	javor [javór]	very, river
[z]	horizont [horizónt]	zebra, please
[ʒ]	kuzhinë [kuʒínə]	forge, pleasure
[θ]	përkthej [pərkθéj]	month, tooth

ABBREVIATIONS
used in the dictionary

English abbreviations

ab.	-	about
adj	-	adjective
adv	-	adverb
anim.	-	animate
as adj	-	attributive noun used as adjective
e.g.	-	for example
etc.	-	et cetera
fam.	-	familiar
fem.	-	feminine
form.	-	formal
inanim.	-	inanimate
masc.	-	masculine
math	-	mathematics
mil.	-	military
n	-	noun
pl	-	plural
pron.	-	pronoun
sb	-	somebody
sing.	-	singular
sth	-	something
v aux	-	auxiliary verb
vi	-	intransitive verb
vi, vt	-	intransitive, transitive verb
vt	-	transitive verb

Albanian abbreviations

f	-	feminine noun
m	-	masculine noun
pl	-	plural

BASIC CONCEPTS

1. Pronouns

I, me	Unë, mua	[unə], [múa]
you	ti, ty	[ti], [ty]
he	ai	[aʃ]
she	ajo	[ajó]
it	ai	[aʃ]
we	ne	[nɛ]
you (to a group)	ju	[ju]
they (masc.)	ata	[atá]
they (fem.)	ato	[ató]

2. Greetings. Salutations

Hello! (fam.)	Përshëndetje!	[pərʃəndétjɛ!]
Hello! (form.)	Përshëndetje!	[pərʃəndétjɛ!]
Good morning!	Mirëmëngjes!	[mirəmənɟés!]
Good afternoon!	Mirëdita!	[mirədíta!]
Good evening!	Mirëmbrëma!	[mirəmbréma!]
to say hello	përshëndes	[pərʃəndés]
Hi! (hello)	Ç'kemi!	[tʃkémi!]
greeting (n)	përshëndetje (f)	[pərʃəndétjɛ]
to greet (vt)	përshëndes	[pərʃəndés]
How are you? (form.)	Si jeni?	[si jéni?]
How are you? (fam.)	Si je?	[si jɛ?]
What's new?	Çfarë ka të re?	[tʃfárə ká tə ré?]
Goodbye!	Mirupafshim!	[mirupáfʃim!]
Bye!	U pafshim!	[u páfʃim!]
See you soon!	Shihemi së shpejti!	[ʃíhɛmi sə ʃpéjti!]
Farewell!	Lamtumirë!	[lamtumírə!]
to say goodbye	përshëndetem	[pərʃəndétɛm]
Cheers!	Tungjatjeta!	[tunɟatjéta!]
Thank you! Cheers!	Faleminderit!	[falɛmindérit!]
Thank you very much!	Faleminderit shumë!	[falɛmindérit ʃúmə!]
My pleasure!	Të lutem	[tə lútɛm]
Don't mention it!	Asgjë!	[asɟé!]
It was nothing	Asgjë	[asɟé]
Excuse me! (fam.)	Më fal!	[mə fal!]
Excuse me! (form.)	Më falni!	[mə fálni!]

to excuse (forgive)	fal	[fal]
to apologize (vi)	kërkoj falje	[kərkój fáljɛ]
My apologies	Kërkoj ndjesë	[kərkój ndjésə]
I'm sorry!	Më vjen keq!	[mə vjɛn kɛc!]
to forgive (vt)	fal	[fal]
It's okay! (that's all right)	S'ka gjë!	[s'ka ɟə!]
please (adv)	të lutem	[tə lútɛm]

Don't forget!	Mos harro!	[mos haró!]
Certainly!	Sigurisht!	[siguríʃt!]
Of course not!	Sigurisht që jo!	[siguríʃt cə jo!]
Okay! (I agree)	Në rregull!	[nə réguɫ!]
That's enough!	Mjafton!	[mjaftón!]

3. Questions

Who?	Kush?	[kuʃ?]
What?	Çka?	[tʃká?]
Where? (at, in)	Ku?	[ku?]
Where (to)?	Për ku?	[pər ku?]
From where?	Nga ku?	[ŋa ku?]
When?	Kur?	[kur?]
Why? (What for?)	Pse?	[psɛ?]
Why? (~ are you crying?)	Pse?	[psɛ?]

What for?	Për çfarë arsye?	[pər tʃfárə arsýɛ?]
How? (in what way)	Si?	[si?]
What? (What kind of ...?)	Çfarë?	[tʃfárə?]
Which?	Cili?	[tsíli?]

To whom?	Kujt?	[kújt?]
About whom?	Për kë?	[pər kə?]
About what?	Për çfarë?	[pər tʃfárə?]
With whom?	Me kë?	[mɛ kə?]

How many? How much?	Sa?	[sa?]
Whose?	Të kujt?	[tə kujt?]

4. Prepositions

with (accompanied by)	me	[mɛ]
without	pa	[pa]
to (indicating direction)	për në	[pər nə]
about (talking ~ ...)	për	[pər]
before (in time)	përpara	[pərpára]
in front of ...	para ...	[pára ...]

under (beneath, below)	nën	[nən]
above (over)	mbi	[mbí]
on (atop)	mbi	[mbí]
from (off, out of)	nga	[ŋa]
of (made from)	nga	[ŋa]

| in (e.g. ~ ten minutes) | për | [pər] |
| over (across the top of) | sipër | [sípər] |

5. Function words. Adverbs. Part 1

Where? (at, in)	Ku?	[ku?]
here (adv)	këtu	[kətú]
there (adv)	atje	[atjé]

| somewhere (to be) | diku | [dikú] |
| nowhere (not in any place) | askund | [askúnd] |

| by (near, beside) | afër | [áfər] |
| by the window | tek dritarja | [tɛk dritárja] |

Where (to)?	Për ku?	[pər ku?]
here (e.g. come ~!)	këtu	[kətú]
there (e.g. to go ~)	atje	[atjé]
from here (adv)	nga këtu	[ŋa kətú]
from there (adv)	nga atje	[ŋa atjɛ]

| close (adv) | pranë | [pránə] |
| far (adv) | larg | [larg] |

near (e.g. ~ Paris)	afër	[áfər]
nearby (adv)	pranë	[pránə]
not far (adv)	jo larg	[jo lárg]

left (adj)	majtë	[májtə]
on the left	majtas	[májtas]
to the left	në të majtë	[nə tə májtə]

right (adj)	djathtë	[djáθtə]
on the right	djathtas	[djáθtas]
to the right	në të djathtë	[nə tə djáθtə]

in front (adv)	përballë	[pərbáłə]
front (as adj)	i përparmë	[i pərpármə]
ahead (the kids ran ~)	përpara	[pərpára]

behind (adv)	prapa	[prápa]
from behind	nga prapa	[ŋa prápa]
back (towards the rear)	pas	[pas]

middle	mes (m)	[mɛs]
in the middle	në mes	[nə mɛs]
at the side	në anë	[nə anə]
everywhere (adv)	kudo	[kúdo]
around (in all directions)	përreth	[pəréθ]

from inside	nga brenda	[ŋa brénda]
somewhere (to go)	diku	[dikú]
straight (directly)	drejt	[dréjt]
back (e.g. come ~)	pas	[pas]

| from anywhere | nga kudo | [ŋa kúdo] |
| from somewhere | nga diku | [ŋa dikú] |

firstly (adv)	së pari	[sə pári]
secondly (adv)	së dyti	[sə dýti]
thirdly (adv)	së treti	[sə tréti]

suddenly (adv)	befas	[béfas]
at first (in the beginning)	në fillim	[nə fiłím]
for the first time	për herë të parë	[pər hérə tə párə]
long before ...	shumë përpara ...	[ʃúmə pərpára ...]
anew (over again)	sërish	[səríʃ]
for good (adv)	një herë e mirë	[ɲə hérə ɛ mírə]

never (adv)	kurrë	[kúrə]
again (adv)	përsëri	[pərsərí]
now (at present)	tani	[táni]
often (adv)	shpesh	[ʃpɛʃ]
then (adv)	atëherë	[atəhérə]
urgently (quickly)	urgjent	[urɟént]
usually (adv)	zakonisht	[zakoníʃt]

by the way, ...	meqë ra fjala, ...	[mécə ra fjála, ...]
possibly	ndoshta	[ndóʃta]
probably (adv)	mundësisht	[mundəsíʃt]
maybe (adv)	mbase	[mbásɛ]
besides ...	përveç	[pərvétʃ]
that's why ...	ja përse ...	[ja pərsé ...]
in spite of ...	pavarësisht se ...	[pavarəsíʃt sɛ ...]
thanks to ...	falë ...	[fálə ...]

what (pron.)	çfarë	[tʃfárə]
that (conj.)	që	[cə]
something	diçka	[ditʃká]
anything (something)	ndonji gjë	[ndoɲí ɟə]
nothing	asgjë	[asɟé]

who (pron.)	kush	[kuʃ]
someone	dikush	[dikúʃ]
somebody	dikush	[dikúʃ]

nobody	askush	[askúʃ]
nowhere (a voyage to ~)	askund	[askúnd]
nobody's	i askujt	[i askújt]
somebody's	i dikujt	[i dikújt]

so (I'm ~ glad)	aq	[ác]
also (as well)	gjithashtu	[ɟiθaʃtú]
too (as well)	gjithashtu	[ɟiθaʃtú]

6. Function words. Adverbs. Part 2

| Why? | Pse? | [psɛ?] |
| for some reason | për një arsye | [pər ɲə arsýɛ] |

| because ... | sepse ... | [sɛpsé ...] |
| for some purpose | për ndonjë shkak | [pər ndóɲə ʃkak] |

and	dhe	[ðɛ]
or	ose	[ósɛ]
but	por	[por]
for (e.g. ~ me)	për	[pər]

too (excessively)	tepër	[tépər]
only (exclusively)	vetëm	[vétəm]
exactly (adv)	pikërisht	[pikəríʃt]
about (more or less)	rreth	[rɛθ]

approximately (adv)	përafërsisht	[pərafərsíʃt]
approximate (adj)	përafërt	[pəráfərt]
almost (adv)	pothuajse	[poθúajsɛ]
the rest	mbetje (f)	[mbétjɛ]

the other (second)	tjetri	[tjétri]
other (different)	tjetër	[tjétər]
each (adj)	çdo	[tʃdo]
any (no matter which)	çfarëdo	[tʃfarədó]
many (adj)	disa	[disá]
much (adv)	shumë	[ʃúmə]
many people	shumë njerëz	[ʃúmə ɲérəz]
all (everyone)	të gjithë	[tə ɟíθə]

in return for ...	në vend të ...	[nə vénd tə ...]
in exchange (adv)	në shkëmbim të ...	[nə ʃkəmbím tə ...]
by hand (made)	me dorë	[mɛ dórə]
hardly (negative opinion)	vështirë se ...	[vəʃtírə sɛ ...]

probably (adv)	mundësisht	[mundəsíʃt]
on purpose (intentionally)	me qëllim	[mɛ cəɫím]
by accident (adv)	aksidentalisht	[aksidɛntalíʃt]

very (adv)	shumë	[ʃúmə]
for example (adv)	për shembull	[pər ʃémbuɫ]
between	midis	[midís]
among	rreth	[rɛθ]
so much (such a lot)	kaq shumë	[kác ʃúmə]
especially (adv)	veçanërisht	[vɛtʃanəríʃt]

NUMBERS. MISCELLANEOUS

7. Cardinal numbers. Part 1

0 zero	zero	[zéro]
1 one	një	[ɲə]
2 two	dy	[dy]
3 three	tre	[trɛ]
4 four	katër	[kátər]
5 five	pesë	[pésə]
6 six	gjashtë	[ʝáʃtə]
7 seven	shtatë	[ʃtátə]
8 eight	tetë	[tétə]
9 nine	nëntë	[nəntə]
10 ten	dhjetë	[ðjétə]
11 eleven	njëmbëdhjetë	[ɲəmbəðjétə]
12 twelve	dymbëdhjetë	[dymbəðjétə]
13 thirteen	trembëdhjetë	[trɛmbəðjétə]
14 fourteen	katërmbëdhjetë	[katərmbəðjétə]
15 fifteen	pesëmbëdhjetë	[pɛsəmbəðjétə]
16 sixteen	gjashtëmbëdhjetë	[ʝaʃtəmbəðjétə]
17 seventeen	shtatëmbëdhjetë	[ʃtatəmbəðjétə]
18 eighteen	tetëmbëdhjetë	[tɛtəmbəðjétə]
19 nineteen	nëntëmbëdhjetë	[nəntəmbəðjétə]
20 twenty	njëzet	[ɲəzét]
21 twenty-one	njëzet e një	[ɲəzét ɛ ɲə]
22 twenty-two	njëzet e dy	[ɲəzét ɛ dy]
23 twenty-three	njëzet e tre	[ɲəzét ɛ trɛ]
30 thirty	tridhjetë	[triðjétə]
31 thirty-one	tridhjetë e një	[triðjétə ɛ ɲə]
32 thirty-two	tridhjetë e dy	[triðjétə ɛ dy]
33 thirty-three	tridhjetë e tre	[triðjétə ɛ trɛ]
40 forty	dyzet	[dyzét]
41 forty-one	dyzet e një	[dyzét ɛ ɲə]
42 forty-two	dyzet e dy	[dyzét ɛ dy]
43 forty-three	dyzet e tre	[dyzét ɛ trɛ]
50 fifty	pesëdhjetë	[pɛsəðjétə]
51 fifty-one	pesëdhjetë e një	[pɛsəðjétə ɛ ɲə]
52 fifty-two	pesëdhjetë e dy	[pɛsəðjétə ɛ dy]
53 fifty-three	pesëdhjetë e tre	[pɛsəðjétə ɛ trɛ]
60 sixty	gjashtëdhjetë	[ʝaʃtəðjétə]
61 sixty-one	gjashtëdhjetë e një	[ʝaʃtəðjétə ɛ ɲə]

| 62 sixty-two | gjashtëdhjetë e dy | [ʝaʃtəðjétə ɛ dý] |
| 63 sixty-three | gjashtëdhjetë e tre | [ʝaʃtəðjétə ɛ tré] |

70 seventy	shtatëdhjetë	[ʃtatəðjétə]
71 seventy-one	shtatëdhjetë e një	[ʃtatəðjétə ɛ ɲə]
72 seventy-two	shtatëdhjetë e dy	[ʃtatəðjétə ɛ dy]
73 seventy-three	shtatëdhjetë e tre	[ʃtatəðjétə ɛ trɛ]

80 eighty	tetëdhjetë	[tɛtəðjétə]
81 eighty-one	tetëdhjetë e një	[tɛtəðjétə ɛ ɲə]
82 eighty-two	tetëdhjetë e dy	[tɛtəðjétə ɛ dy]
83 eighty-three	tetëdhjetë e tre	[tɛtəðjétə ɛ trɛ]

90 ninety	nëntëdhjetë	[nəntəðjétə]
91 ninety-one	nëntëdhjetë e një	[nəntəðjétə ɛ ɲə]
92 ninety-two	nëntëdhjetë e dy	[nəntəðjétə ɛ dy]
93 ninety-three	nëntëdhjetë e tre	[nəntəðjétə ɛ trɛ]

8. Cardinal numbers. Part 2

100 one hundred	njëqind	[ɲəcínd]
200 two hundred	dyqind	[dycínd]
300 three hundred	treqind	[trɛcínd]
400 four hundred	katërqind	[katərcínd]
500 five hundred	pesëqind	[pɛsəcínd]

600 six hundred	gjashtëqind	[ʝaʃtəcínd]
700 seven hundred	shtatëqind	[ʃtatəcínd]
800 eight hundred	tetëqind	[tɛtəcínd]
900 nine hundred	nëntëqind	[nəntəcínd]

1000 one thousand	një mijë	[ɲə míjə]
2000 two thousand	dy mijë	[dy míjə]
3000 three thousand	tre mijë	[trɛ míjə]
10000 ten thousand	dhjetë mijë	[ðjétə míjə]
one hundred thousand	njëqind mijë	[ɲəcínd míjə]
million	milion (m)	[milión]
billion	miliardë (f)	[miliárdə]

9. Ordinal numbers

first (adj)	i pari	[i pári]
second (adj)	i dyti	[i dýti]
third (adj)	i treti	[i tréti]
fourth (adj)	i katërti	[i kátərti]
fifth (adj)	i pesti	[i pésti]

sixth (adj)	i gjashti	[i ʝáʃti]
seventh (adj)	i shtati	[i ʃtáti]
eighth (adj)	i teti	[i téti]
ninth (adj)	i nënti	[i nénti]
tenth (adj)	i dhjeti	[i ðjéti]

COLORS. UNITS OF MEASUREMENT

10. Colours

colour	ngjyrë (f)	[njýrə]
shade (tint)	nuancë (f)	[nuántsə]
hue	tonalitet (m)	[tonalitét]
rainbow	ylber (m)	[ylbér]
white (adj)	e bardhë	[ɛ bárðə]
black (adj)	e zezë	[ɛ zézə]
grey (adj)	gri	[gri]
green (adj)	jeshile	[jɛʃílɛ]
yellow (adj)	e verdhë	[ɛ vérðə]
red (adj)	e kuqe	[ɛ kúcɛ]
blue (adj)	blu	[blu]
light blue (adj)	bojëqielli	[bojəciéłi]
pink (adj)	rozë	[rózə]
orange (adj)	portokalli	[portokáłi]
violet (adj)	bojëvjollcë	[bojəvjółtsə]
brown (adj)	kafe	[káfɛ]
golden (adj)	e artë	[ɛ ártə]
silvery (adj)	e argjendtë	[ɛ arɟéndtə]
beige (adj)	bezhë	[béʒə]
cream (adj)	krem	[krɛm]
turquoise (adj)	e bruztë	[ɛ brúztə]
cherry red (adj)	qershi	[cɛrʃí]
lilac (adj)	jargavan	[jargaván]
crimson (adj)	e kuqe e thellë	[ɛ kúcɛ ɛ θéłə]
light (adj)	e hapur	[ɛ hápur]
dark (adj)	e errët	[ɛ érət]
bright, vivid (adj)	e ndritshme	[ɛ ndrítʃmɛ]
coloured (pencils)	e ngjyrosur	[ɛ njyrósur]
colour (e.g. ~ film)	ngjyrë	[njýrə]
black-and-white (adj)	bardhë e zi	[bárðə ɛ zi]
plain (one-coloured)	njëngjyrëshe	[nənɟýrəʃɛ]
multicoloured (adj)	shumëngjyrëshe	[ʃumənɟýrəʃɛ]

11. Units of measurement

weight	peshë (f)	[péʃə]
length	gjatësi (f)	[ɟatəsí]

width	gjerësi (f)	[ɟɛrəsí]
height	lartësi (f)	[lartəsí]
depth	thellësi (f)	[θɛɫəsí]
volume	vëllim (m)	[vəłím]
area	sipërfaqe (f)	[sipərfácɛ]

gram	gram (m)	[gram]
milligram	miligram (m)	[miligrám]
kilogram	kilogram (m)	[kilográm]
ton	ton (m)	[ton]
pound	paund (m)	[páund]
ounce	ons (m)	[ons]

metre	metër (m)	[métər]
millimetre	milimetër (m)	[milimétər]
centimetre	centimetër (m)	[tsɛntimétər]
kilometre	kilometër (m)	[kilométər]
mile	milje (f)	[míljɛ]

inch	inç (m)	[intʃ]
foot	këmbë (f)	[kə́mbə]
yard	jard (m)	[járd]

square metre	metër katror (m)	[métər katrór]
hectare	hektar (m)	[hɛktár]

litre	litër (m)	[lítər]
degree	gradë (f)	[grádə]
volt	volt (m)	[volt]
ampere	amper (m)	[ampér]
horsepower	kuaj-fuqi (f)	[kúaj-fucí]

quantity	sasi (f)	[sasí]
a little bit of ...	pak ...	[pak ...]
half	gjysmë (f)	[ɟýsmə]
dozen	dyzinë (f)	[dyzínə]
piece (item)	copë (f)	[tsópə]

size	madhësi (f)	[maðəsí]
scale (map ~)	shkallë (f)	[ʃkáłə]

minimal (adj)	minimale	[minimálɛ]
the smallest (adj)	më i vogli	[mə i vógli]
medium (adj)	i mesëm	[i mesəm]
maximal (adj)	maksimale	[maksimálɛ]
the largest (adj)	më i madhi	[mə i máði]

12. Containers

canning jar (glass ~)	kavanoz (m)	[kavanóz]
tin, can	kanoçe (f)	[kanótʃɛ]
bucket	kovë (f)	[kóvə]
barrel	fuçi (f)	[futʃí]
wash basin (e.g., plastic ~)	legen (m)	[lɛgén]

tank (100L water ~)	tank (m)	[taŋk]
hip flask	faqore (f)	[facórɛ]
jerrycan	bidon (m)	[bidón]
tank (e.g., tank car)	cisternë (f)	[tsistérnə]

mug	tas (m)	[tas]
cup (of coffee, etc.)	filxhan (m)	[fildʒán]
saucer	pjatë filxhani (f)	[pjátə fildʒáni]
glass (tumbler)	gotë (f)	[gótə]
wine glass	gotë vere (f)	[gótə vérɛ]
stock pot (soup pot)	tenxhere (f)	[tɛndʒérɛ]

bottle (~ of wine)	shishe (f)	[ʃíʃɛ]
neck (of the bottle, etc.)	grykë	[grýkə]

carafe (decanter)	brokë (f)	[brókə]
pitcher	shtambë (f)	[ʃtámbə]
vessel (container)	enë (f)	[énə]
pot (crock, stoneware ~)	enë (f)	[énə]
vase	vazo (f)	[vázo]

flacon, bottle (perfume ~)	shishe (f)	[ʃíʃɛ]
vial, small bottle	shishkë (f)	[ʃíʃkə]
tube (of toothpaste)	tubet (f)	[tubét]

sack (bag)	thes (m)	[θɛs]
bag (paper ~, plastic ~)	qese (f)	[césɛ]
packet (of cigarettes, etc.)	paketë (f)	[pakétə]

box (e.g. shoebox)	kuti (f)	[kutí]
crate	arkë (f)	[árkə]
basket	shportë (f)	[ʃpórtə]

MAIN VERBS

13. The most important verbs. Part 1

to advise (vt)	këshilloj	[kəʃiɫój]
to agree (say yes)	bie dakord	[bíɛ dakórd]
to answer (vi, vt)	përgjigjem	[pərɟíɟɛm]
to apologize (vi)	kërkoj falje	[kərkój fáljɛ]
to arrive (vi)	arrij	[aríj]
to ask (~ oneself)	pyes	[pýɛs]
to ask (~ sb to do sth)	pyes	[pýɛs]
to be (vi)	jam	[jam]
to be afraid	kam frikë	[kam fríkə]
to be hungry	kam uri	[kam urí]
to be interested in ...	interesohem ...	[intɛrɛsóhɛm ...]
to be needed	nevojitet	[nɛvojítɛt]
to be surprised	çuditem	[tʃudítɛm]
to be thirsty	kam etje	[kam étjɛ]
to begin (vt)	filloj	[fiɫój]
to belong to ...	përkas ...	[pərkás ...]
to boast (vi)	mburrem	[mbúrɛm]
to break (split into pieces)	ndahem	[ndáhɛm]
to call (~ for help)	thërras	[θərás]
can (v aux)	mund	[mund]
to catch (vt)	kap	[kap]
to change (vt)	ndryshoj	[ndryʃój]
to choose (select)	zgjedh	[zɟɛð]
to come down (the stairs)	zbres	[zbrɛs]
to compare (vt)	krahasoj	[krahasój]
to complain (vi, vt)	ankohem	[ankóhɛm]
to confuse (mix up)	ngatërroj	[ŋatərój]
to continue (vt)	vazhdoj	[vaʒdój]
to control (vt)	kontrolloj	[kontroɫój]
to cook (dinner)	gatuaj	[gatúaj]
to cost (vt)	kushton	[kuʃtón]
to count (add up)	numëroj	[numərój]
to count on ...	mbështetem ...	[mbəʃtétɛm ...]
to create (vt)	krijoj	[krijój]
to cry (weep)	qaj	[caj]

14. The most important verbs. Part 2

to deceive (vi, vt)	mashtroj	[maʃtrój]
to decorate (tree, street)	zbukuroj	[zbukurój]

to defend (a country, etc.)	**mbroj**	[mbrój]
to demand (request firmly)	**kërkoj**	[kərkój]
to dig (vt)	**gërmoj**	[gərmój]

to discuss (vt)	**diskutoj**	[diskutój]
to do (vt)	**bëj**	[bəj]
to doubt (have doubts)	**dyshoj**	[dyʃój]
to drop (let fall)	**lëshoj**	[ləʃój]
to enter (room, house, etc.)	**hyj**	[hyj]

to excuse (forgive)	**fal**	[fal]
to exist (vi)	**ekzistoj**	[ɛkzistój]
to expect (foresee)	**parashikoj**	[paraʃikój]
to explain (vt)	**shpjegoj**	[ʃpjɛgój]
to fall (vi)	**bie**	[bíɛ]

to fancy (vt)	**pëlqej**	[pəlcéj]
to find (vt)	**gjej**	[ɟéj]
to finish (vt)	**përfundoj**	[pərfundój]
to fly (vi)	**fluturoj**	[fluturój]
to follow ... (come after)	**ndjek ...**	[ndjék ...]

to forget (vi, vt)	**harroj**	[harój]
to forgive (vt)	**fal**	[fal]
to give (vt)	**jap**	[jap]
to give a hint	**aludoj**	[aludój]
to go (on foot)	**ec në këmbë**	[ɛts nə kémbə]

to go for a swim	**notoj**	[notój]
to go out (for dinner, etc.)	**dal**	[dal]
to guess (the answer)	**hamendësoj**	[hamɛndəsój]

to have (vt)	**kam**	[kam]
to have breakfast	**ha mëngjes**	[ha mənɟés]
to have dinner	**ha darkë**	[ha dárkə]
to have lunch	**ha drekë**	[ha drékə]
to hear (vt)	**dëgjoj**	[dəɟój]

to help (vt)	**ndihmoj**	[ndihmój]
to hide (vt)	**fsheh**	[fʃéh]
to hope (vi, vt)	**shpresoj**	[ʃprɛsój]
to hunt (vi, vt)	**dal për gjah**	[dál pər ɟáh]
to hurry (vi)	**nxitoj**	[ndzitój]

15. The most important verbs. Part 3

to inform (vt)	**informoj**	[informój]
to insist (vi, vt)	**këmbëngul**	[kəmbəŋúl]
to insult (vt)	**fyej**	[fýɛj]
to invite (vt)	**ftoj**	[ftoj]
to joke (vi)	**bëj shaka**	[bəj ʃaká]

to keep (vt)	**mbaj**	[mbáj]
to keep silent, to hush	**hesht**	[hɛʃt]

to kill (vt)	vras	[vras]
to know (sb)	njoh	[ɲóh]
to know (sth)	di	[di]
to laugh (vi)	qesh	[cɛʃ]

to liberate (city, etc.)	çliroj	[tʃlirój]
to look for ... (search)	kërkoj ...	[kərkój ...]
to love (sb)	dashuroj	[daʃurój]
to make a mistake	gaboj	[gabój]
to manage, to run	drejtoj	[drɛjtój]

to mean (signify)	nënkuptoj	[nənkuptój]
to mention (talk about)	përmend	[pərménd]
to miss (school, etc.)	humbas	[humbás]
to notice (see)	vërej	[vəréj]
to object (vi, vt)	kundërshtoj	[kundərʃtój]

to observe (see)	vëzhgoj	[vəʒgój]
to open (vt)	hap	[hap]
to order (meal, etc.)	porosis	[porosís]
to order (mil.)	urdhëroj	[urðərój]
to own (possess)	zotëroj	[zotərój]

to participate (vi)	marr pjesë	[mar pjésə]
to pay (vi, vt)	paguaj	[pagúaj]
to permit (vt)	lejoj	[lɛjój]
to plan (vt)	planifikoj	[planifikój]
to play (children)	luaj	[lúaj]

to pray (vi, vt)	lutem	[lútɛm]
to prefer (vt)	preferoj	[prɛfɛrój]
to promise (vt)	premtoj	[prɛmtój]
to pronounce (vt)	shqiptoj	[ʃciptój]
to propose (vt)	propozoj	[propozój]
to punish (vt)	ndëshkoj	[ndəʃkój]

16. The most important verbs. Part 4

to read (vi, vt)	lexoj	[lɛdzój]
to recommend (vt)	rekomandoj	[rɛkomandój]
to refuse (vi, vt)	refuzoj	[rɛfuzój]
to regret (be sorry)	pendohem	[pɛndóhɛm]
to rent (sth from sb)	marr me qira	[mar mɛ cirá]

to repeat (say again)	përsëris	[pərsərís]
to reserve, to book	rezervoj	[rɛzɛrvój]
to run (vi)	vrapoj	[vrapój]
to save (rescue)	shpëtoj	[ʃpətój]

to say (~ thank you)	them	[θɛm]
to scold (vt)	qortoj	[cortój]
to see (vt)	shikoj	[ʃikój]
to sell (vt)	shes	[ʃɛs]
to send (vt)	dërgoj	[dərgój]

to shoot (vi)	qëlloj	[cətój]
to shout (vi)	bërtas	[bərtás]
to show (vt)	tregoj	[trɛgój]
to sign (document)	nënshkruaj	[nənʃkrúaj]

to sit down (vi)	ulem	[úlɛm]
to smile (vi)	buzëqesh	[buzəcéʃ]
to speak (vi, vt)	flas	[flas]
to steal (money, etc.)	vjedh	[vjɛð]
to stop (for pause, etc.)	ndaloj	[ndalój]

to stop (please ~ calling me)	ndaloj	[ndalój]
to study (vt)	studioj	[studiój]
to swim (vi)	notoj	[notój]
to take (vt)	marr	[mar]
to think (vi, vt)	mendoj	[mɛndój]

to threaten (vt)	kërcënoj	[kərtsənój]
to touch (with hands)	prek	[prɛk]
to translate (vt)	përkthej	[pərkθéj]
to trust (vt)	besoj	[bɛsój]
to try (attempt)	përpiqem	[pərpícɛm]

to turn (e.g., ~ left)	kthej	[kθɛj]
to underestimate (vt)	nënvlerësoj	[nənvlɛrəsój]
to understand (vt)	kuptoj	[kuptój]
to unite (vt)	bashkoj	[baʃkój]
to wait (vt)	pres	[prɛs]

to want (wish, desire)	dëshiroj	[dəʃirój]
to warn (vt)	paralajmëroj	[paralajmərój]
to work (vi)	punoj	[punój]
to write (vt)	shkruaj	[ʃkrúaj]
to write down	mbaj shënim	[mbáj ʃəním]

TIME. CALENDAR

17. Weekdays

Monday	E hënë (f)	[ɛ hénə]
Tuesday	E martë (f)	[ɛ mártə]
Wednesday	E mërkurë (f)	[ɛ mərkúrə]
Thursday	E enjte (f)	[ɛ éɲtɛ]
Friday	E premte (f)	[ɛ prémtɛ]
Saturday	E shtunë (f)	[ɛ ʃtúnə]
Sunday	E dielë (f)	[ɛ díɛlə]

today (adv)	sot	[sot]
tomorrow (adv)	nesër	[nésər]
the day after tomorrow	pasnesër	[pasnésər]
yesterday (adv)	dje	[djé]
the day before yesterday	pardje	[pardjé]

day	ditë (f)	[dítə]
working day	ditë pune (f)	[dítə púnɛ]
public holiday	festë kombëtare (f)	[féstə kombətárɛ]
day off	ditë pushim (m)	[dítə puʃím]
weekend	fundjavë (f)	[fundjávə]

all day long	gjithë ditën	[ɟíθə dítən]
the next day (adv)	ditën pasardhëse	[dítən pasárðəsɛ]
two days ago	dy ditë më parë	[dy dítə mə párə]
the day before	një ditë më parë	[ɲə dítə mə párə]
daily (adj)	ditor	[ditór]
every day (adv)	çdo ditë	[tʃdo dítə]

week	javë (f)	[jávə]
last week (adv)	javën e kaluar	[jávən ɛ kaluar]
next week (adv)	javën e ardhshme	[jávən ɛ árðʃmɛ]
weekly (adj)	javor	[javór]
every week (adv)	çdo javë	[tʃdo jávə]
twice a week	dy herë në javë	[dy hérə nə jávə]
every Tuesday	çdo të martë	[tʃdo tə mártə]

18. Hours. Day and night

morning	mëngjes (m)	[məɲɟés]
in the morning	në mëngjes	[nə məɲɟés]
noon, midday	mesditë (f)	[mɛsdítə]
in the afternoon	pasdite	[pasdítɛ]

evening	mbrëmje (f)	[mbrémjɛ]
in the evening	në mbrëmje	[nə mbrémjɛ]

night	natë (f)	[nátə]
at night	natën	[nátən]
midnight	mesnatë (f)	[mɛsnátə]

second	sekondë (f)	[sɛkóndə]
minute	minutë (f)	[minútə]
hour	orë (f)	[órə]
half an hour	gjysmë ore (f)	[ɟýsmə órɛ]
a quarter-hour	çerek ore (m)	[tʃɛrék órɛ]
fifteen minutes	pesëmbëdhjetë minuta	[pɛsəmbəðjétə minúta]
24 hours	24 orë	[nəzét ɛ kátər órə]

sunrise	agim (m)	[agím]
dawn	agim (m)	[agím]
early morning	mëngjes herët (m)	[mənɟés hérət]
sunset	perëndim dielli (m)	[pɛrəndím diéɫi]

early in the morning	herët në mëngjes	[hérət nə mənɟés]
this morning	sot në mëngjes	[sot nə mənɟés]
tomorrow morning	nesër në mëngjes	[nésər nə mənɟés]

this afternoon	sot pasdite	[sot pasdítɛ]
in the afternoon	pasdite	[pasdítɛ]
tomorrow afternoon	nesër pasdite	[nésər pasdítɛ]

tonight (this evening)	sonte në mbrëmje	[sóntɛ nə mbrəmjɛ]
tomorrow night	nesër në mbrëmje	[nésər nə mbrémjɛ]

at 3 o'clock sharp	në orën 3 fiks	[nə órən trɛ fiks]
about 4 o'clock	rreth orës 4	[rɛθ órəs kátər]
by 12 o'clock	deri në orën 12	[déri nə órən dymbəðjétə]

in 20 minutes	për 20 minuta	[pər nəzét minúta]
in an hour	për një orë	[pər ɲə órə]
on time (adv)	në orar	[nə orár]

a quarter to …	çerek …	[tʃɛrék …]
within an hour	brenda një ore	[brénda ɲə órɛ]
every 15 minutes	çdo 15 minuta	[tʃdo pɛsəmbəðjétə minúta]
round the clock	gjithë ditën	[ɟíθə dítən]

19. Months. Seasons

January	Janar (m)	[janár]
February	Shkurt (m)	[ʃkurt]
March	Mars (m)	[mars]
April	Prill (m)	[priɫ]
May	Maj (m)	[maj]
June	Qershor (m)	[cɛrʃór]

July	Korrik (m)	[korík]
August	Gusht (m)	[guʃt]
September	Shtator (m)	[ʃtatór]
October	Tetor (m)	[tɛtór]

| November | Nëntor (m) | [nəntór] |
| December | Dhjetor (m) | [ðjɛtór] |

spring	pranverë (f)	[pranvérə]
in spring	në pranverë	[nə pranvérə]
spring (as adj)	pranveror	[pranvɛrór]

summer	verë (f)	[vérə]
in summer	në verë	[nə vérə]
summer (as adj)	veror	[vɛrór]

autumn	vjeshtë (f)	[vjéʃtə]
in autumn	në vjeshtë	[nə vjéʃtə]
autumn (as adj)	vjeshtor	[vjéʃtor]

winter	dimër (m)	[dímər]
in winter	në dimër	[nə dímər]
winter (as adj)	dimëror	[dimərór]

month	muaj (m)	[múaj]
this month	këtë muaj	[kətə múaj]
next month	muajin tjetër	[múajin tjétər]
last month	muajin e kaluar	[múajin ɛ kalúar]

a month ago	para një muaji	[pára ɲə múaji]
in a month (a month later)	pas një muaji	[pas ɲə múaji]
in 2 months (2 months later)	pas dy muajsh	[pas dy múajʃ]
the whole month	gjithë muajin	[ɟíθə múajin]
all month long	gjatë gjithë muajit	[ɟátə ɟíθə múajit]

monthly (~ magazine)	mujor	[mujór]
monthly (adv)	mujor	[mujór]
every month	çdo muaj	[tʃdo múaj]
twice a month	dy herë në muaj	[dy hérə nə múaj]

year	vit (m)	[vit]
this year	këtë vit	[kətə vít]
next year	vitin tjetër	[vítin tjétər]
last year	vitin e kaluar	[vítin ɛ kalúar]

a year ago	para një viti	[pára ɲə víti]
in a year	për një vit	[pər ɲə vit]
in two years	për dy vite	[pər dy vítɛ]
the whole year	gjithë vitin	[ɟíθə vítin]
all year long	gjatë gjithë vitit	[ɟátə ɟíθə vítit]

every year	çdo vit	[tʃdo vít]
annual (adj)	vjetor	[vjɛtór]
annually (adv)	çdo vit	[tʃdo vít]
4 times a year	4 herë në vit	[kátər hérə nə vit]

date (e.g. today's ~)	datë (f)	[dátə]
date (e.g. ~ of birth)	data (f)	[dáta]
calendar	kalendar (m)	[kalɛndár]
half a year	gjysmë viti	[ɟýsmə víti]
six months	gjashtë muaj	[ɟáʃtə múaj]

season (summer, etc.)	**stinë** (f)	[stínə]
century	**shekull** (m)	[ʃékuɫ]

TRAVEL. HOTEL

20. Trip. Travel

tourism, travel	turizëm (m)	[turízəm]
tourist	turist (m)	[turíst]
trip, voyage	udhëtim (m)	[uðətím]
adventure	aventurë (f)	[avɛntúrə]
trip, journey	udhëtim (m)	[uðətím]
holiday	pushim (m)	[puʃím]
to be on holiday	jam me pushime	[jam mɛ puʃímɛ]
rest	pushim (m)	[puʃím]
train	tren (m)	[trɛn]
by train	me tren	[mɛ trén]
aeroplane	avion (m)	[avión]
by aeroplane	me avion	[mɛ avión]
by car	me makinë	[mɛ makínə]
by ship	me anije	[mɛ aníjɛ]
luggage	bagazh (m)	[bagáʒ]
suitcase	valixhe (f)	[valídʒɛ]
luggage trolley	karrocë bagazhesh (f)	[karótsə bagáʒɛʃ]
passport	pasaportë (f)	[pasapórtə]
visa	vizë (f)	[vízə]
ticket	biletë (f)	[bilétə]
air ticket	biletë avioni (f)	[bilétə avióni]
guidebook	guidë turistike (f)	[guídə turistíkɛ]
map (tourist ~)	hartë (f)	[hártə]
area (rural ~)	zonë (f)	[zónə]
place, site	vend (m)	[vɛnd]
exotica (n)	ekzotikë (f)	[ɛkzotíkə]
exotic (adj)	ekzotik	[ɛkzotík]
amazing (adj)	mahnitëse	[mahnítəsɛ]
group	grup (m)	[grup]
excursion, sightseeing tour	ekskursion (m)	[ɛkskursión]
guide (person)	udhërrëfyes (m)	[uðərəfýɛs]

21. Hotel

hotel	hotel (m)	[hotél]
motel	motel (m)	[motél]
three-star (~ hotel)	me tre yje	[mɛ trɛ ýjɛ]

five-star	me pesë yje	[mɛ pésə ýjɛ]
to stay (in a hotel, etc.)	qëndroj	[cəndrój]

room	dhomë (f)	[ðómə]
single room	dhomë teke (f)	[ðómə tékɛ]
double room	dhomë dyshe (f)	[ðómə dýʃɛ]
to book a room	rezervoj një dhomë	[rɛzɛrvój ɲə ðómə]

half board	gjysmë-pension (m)	[ɟýsmə-pɛnsión]
full board	pension i plotë (m)	[pɛnsión i plótə]

with bath	me banjo	[mɛ báɲo]
with shower	me dush	[mɛ dúʃ]
satellite television	televizor satelitor (m)	[tɛlɛvizór satɛlitór]
air-conditioner	kondicioner (m)	[konditsionér]
towel	peshqir (m)	[pɛʃcír]
key	çelës (m)	[tʃéləs]

administrator	administrator (m)	[administratór]
chambermaid	pastruese (f)	[pastrúɛsɛ]
porter	portier (m)	[portiér]
doorman	portier (m)	[portiér]

restaurant	restorant (m)	[rɛstoránt]
pub, bar	pab (m), pijetore (f)	[pab], [pijɛtórɛ]
breakfast	mëngjes (m)	[mənɟés]
dinner	darkë (f)	[dárkə]
buffet	bufe (f)	[bufé]

lobby	holl (m)	[hoɫ]
lift	ashensor (m)	[aʃɛnsór]

DO NOT DISTURB	MOS SHQETËSONI	[mos ʃcɛtəsóni]
NO SMOKING	NDALOHET DUHANI	[ndalóhɛt duháni]

22. Sightseeing

monument	monument (m)	[monumént]
fortress	kala (f)	[kalá]
palace	pallat (m)	[paɫát]
castle	kështjellë (f)	[kəʃtjéɫə]
tower	kullë (f)	[kúɫə]
mausoleum	mauzoleum (m)	[mauzolɛúm]

architecture	arkitekturë (f)	[arkitɛktúrə]
medieval (adj)	mesjetare	[mɛsjɛtárɛ]
ancient (adj)	e lashtë	[ɛ láʃtə]
national (adj)	kombëtare	[kombətárɛ]
famous (monument, etc.)	i famshëm	[i fámʃəm]

tourist	turist (m)	[turíst]
guide (person)	udhërrëfyes (m)	[uðərəfýɛs]
excursion, sightseeing tour	ekskursion (m)	[ɛkskursión]
to show (vt)	tregoj	[trɛgój]

to tell (vt)	**dëftoj**	[dəftój]
to find (vt)	**gjej**	[ɟéj]
to get lost (lose one's way)	**humbas**	[humbás]
map (e.g. underground ~)	**hartë** (f)	[hártə]
map (e.g. city ~)	**hartë** (f)	[hártə]
souvenir, gift	**suvenir** (m)	[suvɛnír]
gift shop	**dyqan dhuratash** (m)	[dycán ðurátaʃ]
to take pictures	**bëj foto**	[bəj fóto]
to have one's picture taken	**bëj fotografi**	[bəj fotografí]

TRANSPORT

23. Airport

airport	**aeroport** (m)	[aɛropórt]
aeroplane	**avion** (m)	[avión]
airline	**kompani ajrore** (f)	[kompaní ajrórɛ]
air traffic controller	**kontroll i trafikut ajror** (m)	[kontróɫ i trafíkut ajrór]
departure	**nisje** (f)	[nísjɛ]
arrival	**arritje** (f)	[arítjɛ]
to arrive (by plane)	**arrij me avion**	[aríj mɛ avión]
departure time	**nisja** (f)	[nísja]
arrival time	**arritja** (f)	[arítja]
to be delayed	**vonesë**	[vonésə]
flight delay	**vonesë avioni** (f)	[vonésə avióni]
information board	**ekrani i informacioneve** (m)	[ɛkráni i informatsiónɛvɛ]
information	**informacion** (m)	[informatsión]
to announce (vt)	**njoftoj**	[ɲoftój]
flight (e.g. next ~)	**fluturim** (m)	[fluturím]
customs	**doganë** (f)	[dogánə]
customs officer	**doganier** (m)	[doganiér]
customs declaration	**deklarim doganor** (m)	[dɛklarím doganór]
to fill in (vt)	**plotësoj**	[plotəsój]
to fill in the declaration	**plotësoj deklaratën**	[plotəsój dɛklarátən]
passport control	**kontroll pasaportash** (m)	[kontróɫ pasapórtaʃ]
luggage	**bagazh** (m)	[bagáʒ]
hand luggage	**bagazh dore** (m)	[bagáʒ dórɛ]
luggage trolley	**karrocë bagazhesh** (f)	[karótsə bagáʒɛʃ]
landing	**aterrim** (m)	[atɛrím]
landing strip	**pistë aterrimi** (f)	[pístə atɛrími]
to land (vi)	**aterroj**	[atɛrój]
airstair (passenger stair)	**shkallë avioni** (f)	[ʃkáɫə avióni]
check-in	**regjistrim** (m)	[rɛɟistrím]
check-in counter	**sportel regjistrimi** (m)	[sportél rɛɟistrími]
to check-in (vi)	**regjistrohem**	[rɛɟistróhɛm]
boarding card	**biletë e hyrjes** (f)	[bilétə ɛ hýrjɛs]
departure gate	**porta e nisjes** (f)	[pórta ɛ nísjɛs]
transit	**transit** (m)	[transít]
to wait (vt)	**pres**	[prɛs]
departure lounge	**salla e nisjes** (f)	[sáɫa ɛ nísjɛs]

| to see off | përcjell | [pərtsjéɫ] |
| to say goodbye | përshëndetem | [pərʃəndétɛm] |

24. Aeroplane

aeroplane	avion (m)	[avión]
air ticket	biletë avioni (f)	[bilétə avióni]
airline	kompani ajrore (f)	[kompaní ajrórɛ]
airport	aeroport (m)	[aɛropórt]
supersonic (adj)	supersonik	[supɛrsoník]

captain	kapiten (m)	[kapitén]
crew	ekip (m)	[ɛkíp]
pilot	pilot (m)	[pilót]
stewardess	stjuardesë (f)	[stjuardésə]
navigator	navigues (m)	[navigúɛs]

wings	krahë (pl)	[kráhə]
tail	bisht (m)	[biʃt]
cockpit	kabinë (f)	[kabínə]
engine	motor (m)	[motór]
undercarriage (landing gear)	karrel (m)	[karél]
turbine	turbinë (f)	[turbínə]
propeller	helikë (f)	[hɛlíkə]
black box	kuti e zezë (f)	[kutí ɛ zézə]
yoke (control column)	timon (m)	[timón]
fuel	karburant (m)	[karburánt]

safety card	udhëzime sigurie (pl)	[uðəzímɛ siguríɛ]
oxygen mask	maskë oksigjeni (f)	[máskə oksiɟéni]
uniform	uniformë (f)	[unifórmə]
lifejacket	jelek shpëtimi (m)	[jɛlék ʃpətími]
parachute	parashutë (f)	[paraʃútə]
takeoff	ngritje (f)	[ŋrítjɛ]
to take off (vi)	fluturon	[fluturón]
runway	pista e fluturimit (f)	[písta ɛ fluturímit]

visibility	shikueshmëri (f)	[ʃikuɛʃmərí]
flight (act of flying)	fluturim (m)	[fluturím]
altitude	lartësi (f)	[lartəsí]
air pocket	xhep ajri (m)	[dʒɛp ájri]

seat	karrige (f)	[karígɛ]
headphones	kufje (f)	[kúfjɛ]
folding tray (tray table)	tabaka (f)	[tabaká]
airplane window	dritare avioni (f)	[dritárɛ avióni]
aisle	korridor (m)	[koridór]

25. Train

| train | tren (m) | [trɛn] |
| commuter train | tren elektrik (m) | [trɛn ɛlɛktrík] |

express train	tren ekspres (m)	[trɛn ɛksprés]
diesel locomotive	lokomotivë me naftë (f)	[lokomótivə mɛ náftə]
steam locomotive	lokomotivë me avull (f)	[lokomótivə mɛ ávuɫ]

| coach, carriage | vagon (m) | [vagón] |
| buffet car | vagon restorant (m) | [vagón rɛstoránt] |

rails	shina (pl)	[ʃína]
railway	hekurudhë (f)	[hɛkurúðə]
sleeper (track support)	traversë (f)	[travérsə]

platform (railway ~)	platformë (f)	[platfórmə]
platform (~ 1, 2, etc.)	binar (m)	[binár]
semaphore	semafor (m)	[sɛmafór]
station	stacion (m)	[statsión]
train driver	makinist (m)	[makiníst]
porter (of luggage)	portier (m)	[portiér]
carriage attendant	konduktor (m)	[konduktór]
passenger	pasagjer (m)	[pasaɟér]
ticket inspector	konduktor (m)	[konduktór]

| corridor (in train) | korridor (m) | [koridór] |
| emergency brake | frena urgjence (f) | [fréna urɟéntsɛ] |

compartment	ndarje (f)	[ndárjɛ]
berth	kat (m)	[kat]
upper berth	kati i sipërm (m)	[káti i sípərm]
lower berth	kati i poshtëm (m)	[káti i póʃtəm]
bed linen, bedding	shtroje shtrati (pl)	[ʃtrójɛ ʃtráti]
ticket	biletë (f)	[bilétə]
timetable	orar (m)	[orár]
information display	tabelë e informatave (f)	[tabélə ɛ informátavɛ]

to leave, to depart	niset	[nísɛt]
departure (of a train)	nisje (f)	[nísjɛ]
to arrive (ab. train)	arrij	[aríj]
arrival	arritje (f)	[arítjɛ]

to arrive by train	arrij me tren	[aríj mɛ trɛn]
to get on the train	hip në tren	[hip nə trén]
to get off the train	zbres nga treni	[zbrɛs ŋa tréni]

| train crash | aksident hekurudhor (m) | [aksidént hɛkuruðór] |
| to derail (vi) | del nga shinat | [dɛl ŋa ʃínat] |

steam locomotive	lokomotivë me avull (f)	[lokomótivə mɛ ávuɫ]
stoker, fireman	mbikëqyrës i zjarrit (m)	[mbikəcýrəs i zjárit]
firebox	furrë (f)	[fúrə]
coal	qymyr (m)	[cymýr]

26. Ship

| ship | anije (f) | [aníjɛ] |
| vessel | mjet lundrues (m) | [mjét lundrúɛs] |

steamship	anije me avull (f)	[aníjɛ mɛ ávuɬ]
riverboat	anije lumi (f)	[aníjɛ lúmi]
cruise ship	krocierë (f)	[krotsiérə]
cruiser	anije luftarake (f)	[aníjɛ luftarákɛ]

yacht	jaht (m)	[jáht]
tugboat	anije rimorkiuese (f)	[aníjɛ rimorkiúɛsɛ]
barge	anije transportuese (f)	[aníjɛ transportúɛsɛ]
ferry	traget (m)	[tragét]

| sailing ship | anije me vela (f) | [aníjɛ mɛ véla] |
| brigantine | brigantinë (f) | [brigantínə] |

| ice breaker | akullthyese (f) | [akuɬθýɛsɛ] |
| submarine | nëndetëse (f) | [nəndétəsɛ] |

boat (flat-bottomed ~)	barkë (f)	[bárkə]
dinghy (lifeboat)	gomone (f)	[gomónɛ]
lifeboat	varkë shpëtimi (f)	[várkə ʃpətími]
motorboat	skaf (m)	[skaf]

captain	kapiten (m)	[kapitén]
seaman	marinar (m)	[marinár]
sailor	marinar (m)	[marinár]
crew	ekip (m)	[ɛkíp]

boatswain	kryemarinar (m)	[kryɛmarinár]
ship's boy	djali i anijes (m)	[djáli i aníjɛs]
cook	kuzhinier (m)	[kuʒiniér]
ship's doctor	doktori i anijes (m)	[doktóri i aníjɛs]

deck	kuverta (f)	[kuvérta]
mast	direk (m)	[dirék]
sail	vela (f)	[véla]

hold	bagazh (m)	[bagáʒ]
bow (prow)	harku sipëror (m)	[hárku sipərór]
stern	pjesa e pasme (f)	[pjésa ɛ pásmɛ]
oar	rrem (m)	[rɛm]
screw propeller	helikë (f)	[hɛlíkə]

cabin	kabinë (f)	[kabínə]
wardroom	zyrë e oficerëve (m)	[zýrə ɛ ofitsérəvɛ]
engine room	salla e motorit (m)	[sáɬa ɛ motórit]
bridge	urë komanduese (f)	[úrə komandúɛsɛ]
radio room	kabina radiotelegrafike (f)	[kabína radiotɛlɛgrafíkɛ]
wave (radio)	valë (f)	[válə]
logbook	libri i shënimeve (m)	[líbri i ʃənímɛvɛ]

spyglass	dylbi (f)	[dylbí]
bell	këmbanë (f)	[kəmbánə]
flag	flamur (m)	[flamúr]

hawser (mooring ~)	pallamar (m)	[paɬamár]
knot (bowline, etc.)	nyjë (f)	[nýjə]
deckrails	parmakë (pl)	[parmákə]

gangway	shkallë (f)	[ʃkátə]
anchor	spirancë (f)	[spirántsə]
to weigh anchor	ngre spirancën	[ŋré spirántsən]
to drop anchor	hedh spirancën	[hɛð spirántsən]
anchor chain	zinxhir i spirancës (m)	[zindʒír i spirántsəs]

port (harbour)	port (m)	[port]
quay, wharf	skelë (f)	[skélə]
to berth (moor)	ankoroj	[ankorój]
to cast off	niset	[nísɛt]

trip, voyage	udhëtim (m)	[uðətím]
cruise (sea trip)	udhëtim me krocierë (f)	[uðətím mɛ krotsiérə]
course (route)	kursi i udhëtimit (m)	[kúrsi i uðətímit]
route (itinerary)	itinerar (m)	[itinɛrár]

fairway (safe water channel)	ujëra të lundrueshme (f)	[újəra tə lundrúɛʃmɛ]
shallows	cekëtinë (f)	[tsɛkətínə]
to run aground	bllokohet në rërë	[błokóhɛt nə rərə]

storm	stuhi (f)	[stuhí]
signal	sinjal (m)	[siɲál]
to sink (vi)	fundoset	[fundósɛt]
Man overboard!	Njeri në det!	[ɲɛrí nə dɛt!]
SOS (distress signal)	SOS (m)	[sos]
ring buoy	bovë shpëtuese (f)	[bóvə ʃpətúɛsɛ]

CITY

bus, coach	autobus (m)	[autobús]
tram	tramvaj (m)	[tramváj]
trolleybus	autobus tramvaj (m)	[autobús tramváj]
route (bus ~)	itinerar (m)	[itinɛrár]
number (e.g. bus ~)	numër (m)	[númər]

to go by ...	udhëtoj me ...	[uðətój mɛ ...]
to get on (~ the bus)	hip	[hip]
to get off ...	zbres ...	[zbrɛs ...]

stop (e.g. bus ~)	stacion (m)	[statsión]
next stop	stacioni tjetër (m)	[statsióni tjétər]
terminus	terminal (m)	[tɛrminál]
timetable	orar (m)	[orár]
to wait (vt)	pres	[prɛs]

| ticket | biletë (f) | [bilétə] |
| fare | çmim bilete (m) | [tʃmím bilétɛ] |

cashier (ticket seller)	shitës biletash (m)	[ʃítəs bilétaʃ]
ticket inspection	kontroll biletash (m)	[kontróɫ bilétaʃ]
ticket inspector	kontrollues biletash (m)	[kontroɫúɛs bilétaʃ]

to be late (for ...)	vonohem	[vonóhɛm]
to miss (~ the train, etc.)	humbas	[humbás]
to be in a hurry	nxitoj	[ndzitój]

taxi, cab	taksi (m)	[táksi]
taxi driver	shofer taksie (m)	[ʃofér taksíɛ]
by taxi	me taksi	[mɛ táksi]
taxi rank	stacion taksish (m)	[statsión táksiʃ]
to call a taxi	thërras taksi	[θərás táksi]
to take a taxi	marr taksi	[mar táksi]

traffic	trafik (m)	[trafík]
traffic jam	bllokim trafiku (m)	[bɫokím trafíku]
rush hour	orë e trafikut të rëndë (f)	[órə ɛ trafikut tə rəndə]
to park (vi)	parkoj	[parkój]
to park (vt)	parkim	[parkím]
car park	parking (m)	[parkíŋ]

underground, tube	metro (f)	[mɛtró]
station	stacion (m)	[statsión]
to take the tube	shkoj me metro	[ʃkoj mɛ métro]
train	tren (m)	[trɛn]
train station	stacion treni (m)	[statsión tréni]

28. City. Life in the city

city, town	qytet (m)	[cytét]
capital city	kryeqytet (m)	[kryεcytét]
village	fshat (m)	[fʃát]
city map	hartë e qytetit (f)	[hártə ε cytétit]
city centre	qendër e qytetit (f)	[céndər ε cytétit]
suburb	periferi (f)	[pεrifεrí]
suburban (adj)	periferik	[pεrifεrík]
outskirts	periferia (f)	[pεrifεría]
environs (suburbs)	periferia (f)	[pεrifεría]
city block	bllok pallatesh (m)	[bɫók paɫátεʃ]
residential block (area)	bllok banimi (m)	[bɫók baními]
traffic	trafik (m)	[trafík]
traffic lights	semafor (m)	[sεmafór]
public transport	transport publik (m)	[transpórt publík]
crossroads	kryqëzim (m)	[krycəzím]
zebra crossing	kalim për këmbësorë (m)	[kalím pər kəmbəsórə]
pedestrian subway	nënkalim për këmbësorë (m)	[nənkalím pər kəmbəsórə]
to cross (~ the street)	kapërcej	[kapərtséj]
pedestrian	këmbësor (m)	[kəmbəsór]
pavement	trotuar (m)	[trotuár]
bridge	urë (f)	[úrə]
embankment (river walk)	breg lumi (m)	[brεg lúmi]
fountain	shatërvan (m)	[ʃatərván]
allée (garden walkway)	rrugëz (m)	[rúgəz]
park	park (m)	[park]
boulevard	bulevard (m)	[bulεvárd]
square	shesh (m)	[ʃεʃ]
avenue (wide street)	bulevard (m)	[bulεvárd]
street	rrugë (f)	[rúgə]
side street	rrugë dytësore (f)	[rúgə dytəsórε]
dead end	rrugë pa krye (f)	[rúgə pa krýε]
house	shtëpi (f)	[ʃtəpí]
building	ndërtesë (f)	[ndərtésə]
skyscraper	qiellgërvishtës (m)	[ciεɫgərvíʃtəs]
facade	fasadë (f)	[fasádə]
roof	çati (f)	[tʃatí]
window	dritare (f)	[dritárε]
arch	hark (m)	[hárk]
column	kolonë (f)	[kolónə]
corner	kënd (m)	[kénd]
shop window	vitrinë (f)	[vitrínə]
signboard (store sign, etc.)	tabelë (f)	[tabélə]
poster (e.g., playbill)	poster (m)	[postér]
advertising poster	afishe reklamuese (f)	[afíʃε rεklamúεsε]

hoarding	tabelë reklamash (f)	[tabélə rɛklámaʃ]
rubbish	plehra (f)	[pléhra]
rubbish bin	kosh plehrash (m)	[koʃ pléhraʃ]
to litter (vi)	hedh mbeturina	[hɛð mbɛturína]
rubbish dump	deponi plehrash (f)	[dɛponí pléhraʃ]
telephone box	kabinë telefonike (f)	[kabínə tɛlɛfoníkɛ]
lamppost	shtyllë dritash (f)	[ʃtýłə drítaʃ]
bench (park ~)	stol (m)	[stol]
police officer	polic (m)	[políts]
police	polici (f)	[politsí]
beggar	lypës (m)	[lýpəs]
homeless (n)	i pastrehë (m)	[i pastréhə]

29. Urban institutions

shop	dyqan (m)	[dycán]
chemist, pharmacy	farmaci (f)	[farmatsí]
optician (spectacles shop)	optikë (f)	[optíkə]
shopping centre	qendër tregtare (f)	[céndər trɛgtárɛ]
supermarket	supermarket (m)	[supɛrmarkét]
bakery	furrë (f)	[fúrə]
baker	furrtar (m)	[furtár]
cake shop	pastiçeri (f)	[pastitʃɛrí]
grocery shop	dyqan ushqimor (m)	[dycán uʃcimór]
butcher shop	dyqan mishi (m)	[dycán míʃi]
greengrocer	dyqan fruta-perimesh (m)	[dycán frúta-pɛrímɛʃ]
market	treg (m)	[trɛg]
coffee bar	kafene (f)	[kafɛné]
restaurant	restorant (m)	[rɛstoránt]
pub, bar	pab (m), pijetore (f)	[pab], [pijɛtórɛ]
pizzeria	piceri (f)	[pitsɛrí]
hairdresser	parukeri (f)	[parukɛrí]
post office	zyrë postare (f)	[zýrə postárɛ]
dry cleaners	pastrim kimik (m)	[pastrím kimík]
photo studio	studio fotografike (f)	[stúdio fotografíkɛ]
shoe shop	dyqan këpucësh (m)	[dycán kəpútsəʃ]
bookshop	librari (f)	[librarí]
sports shop	dyqan me mallra sportivë (m)	[dycán mɛ máłra sportívə]
clothes repair shop	rrobaqepësi (f)	[robacɛpəsí]
formal wear hire	dyqan veshjesh me qira (m)	[dycán véʃjeʃ mɛ cirá]
video rental shop	dyqan videosh me qira (m)	[dycán vídeoʃ mɛ cirá]
circus	cirk (m)	[tsírk]
zoo	kopsht zoologjik (m)	[kópʃt zooloɟík]
cinema	kinema (f)	[kinɛmá]

| museum | muze (m) | [muzé] |
| library | bibliotekë (f) | [bibliotékə] |

theatre	teatër (m)	[tɛátər]
opera (opera house)	opera (f)	[opéra]
nightclub	klub nate (m)	[klúb nátɛ]
casino	kazino (f)	[kazíno]

mosque	xhami (f)	[dʒamí]
synagogue	sinagogë (f)	[sinagógə]
cathedral	katedrale (f)	[katɛdrálɛ]
temple	tempull (m)	[témpuł]
church	kishë (f)	[kíʃə]

college	kolegj (m)	[koléɟ]
university	universitet (m)	[univɛrsitét]
school	shkollë (f)	[ʃkółə]

prefecture	prefekturë (f)	[prɛfɛktúrə]
town hall	bashki (f)	[baʃkí]
hotel	hotel (m)	[hotél]
bank	bankë (f)	[bánkə]

embassy	ambasadë (f)	[ambasádə]
travel agency	agjenci udhëtimesh (f)	[aɟɛntsí uðətímɛʃ]
information office	zyrë informacioni (f)	[zýrə informatsióni]
currency exchange	këmbim valutor (m)	[kəmbím valutór]

| underground, tube | metro (f) | [mɛtró] |
| hospital | spital (m) | [spitál] |

| petrol station | pikë karburanti (f) | [píkə karburánti] |
| car park | parking (m) | [parkíŋ] |

30. Signs

signboard (store sign, etc.)	tabelë (f)	[tabélə]
notice (door sign, etc.)	njoftim (m)	[ɲoftím]
poster	poster (m)	[postér]
direction sign	tabelë drejtuese (f)	[tabélə drɛjtúɛsɛ]
arrow (sign)	shigjetë (f)	[ʃiɟétə]

caution	kujdes (m)	[kujdés]
warning sign	shenjë paralajmëruese (f)	[ʃéɲə paralajmərúɛsɛ]
to warn (vt)	paralajmëroj	[paralajmərój]

rest day (weekly ~)	ditë pushimi (f)	[dítə puʃími]
timetable (schedule)	orar (m)	[orár]
opening hours	orari i punës (m)	[orári i púnəs]

WELCOME!	MIRË SE VINI!	[mírə sɛ víni!]
ENTRANCE	HYRJE	[hýrjɛ]
WAY OUT	DALJE	[dáljɛ]
PUSH	SHTY	[ʃty]

PULL	TËRHIQ	[tərhíc]
OPEN	HAPUR	[hápur]
CLOSED	MBYLLUR	[mbýɫur]

| WOMEN | GRA | [gra] |
| MEN | BURRA | [búra] |

DISCOUNTS	ZBRITJE	[zbrítjɛ]
SALE	ULJE	[úljɛ]
NEW!	TË REJA!	[tə réja!]
FREE	FALAS	[fálas]

ATTENTION!	KUJDES!	[kujdés!]
NO VACANCIES	NUK KA VENDE TË LIRA	[nuk ka véndɛ tə líra]
RESERVED	E REZERVUAR	[ɛ rɛzɛrvúar]

| ADMINISTRATION | ADMINISTRATA | [administráta] |
| STAFF ONLY | VETËM PËR STAFIN | [vétəm pər stáfin] |

BEWARE OF THE DOG!	RUHUNI NGA QENI!	[rúhuni ŋa céni!]
NO SMOKING	NDALOHET DUHANI	[ndalóhɛt duháni]
DO NOT TOUCH!	MOS PREK!	[mos prék!]

DANGEROUS	TË RREZIKSHME	[tə rɛzíkʃmɛ]
DANGER	RREZIK	[rɛzík]
HIGH VOLTAGE	TENSION I LARTË	[tɛnsión i lártə]
NO SWIMMING!	NUK LEJOHET NOTI!	[nuk lɛjóhɛt nóti!]
OUT OF ORDER	E PRISHUR	[ɛ príʃur]

FLAMMABLE	LËNDË DJEGËSE	[ləndə djégəsɛ]
FORBIDDEN	E NDALUAR	[ɛ ndalúar]
NO TRESPASSING!	NDALOHET HYRJA	[ndalóhɛt hýrja]
WET PAINT	BOJË E FRESKËT	[bójə ɛ fréskət]

31. Shopping

to buy (purchase)	blej	[blɛj]
shopping	blerje (f)	[blérjɛ]
to go shopping	shkoj për pazar	[ʃkoj pər pazár]
shopping	pazar (m)	[pazár]

| to be open (ab. shop) | hapur | [hápur] |
| to be closed | mbyllur | [mbýɫur] |

footwear, shoes	këpucë (f)	[kəpútsə]
clothes, clothing	veshje (f)	[véʃjɛ]
cosmetics	kozmetikë (f)	[kozmɛtíkə]
food products	mallra ushqimore (f)	[máɫra uʃcimórɛ]
gift, present	dhuratë (f)	[ðurátə]

shop assistant (masc.)	shitës (m)	[ʃítəs]
shop assistant (fem.)	shitëse (f)	[ʃítəsɛ]
cash desk	arkë (f)	[árkə]
mirror	pasqyrë (f)	[pascýrə]

| counter (shop ~) | banak (m) | [bának] |
| fitting room | dhomë prove (f) | [ðómə próvɛ] |

to try on	provoj	[provój]
to fit (ab. dress, etc.)	më rri mirë	[mə ri mírə]
to fancy (vt)	pëlqej	[pəlcéj]

price	çmim (m)	[tʃmím]
price tag	etiketa e çmimit (f)	[ɛtikéta ɛ tʃmímit]
to cost (vt)	kushton	[kuʃtón]
How much?	Sa?	[sa?]
discount	ulje (f)	[úljɛ]

inexpensive (adj)	jo e shtrenjtë	[jo ɛ ʃtréɲtə]
cheap (adj)	e lirë	[ɛ lírə]
expensive (adj)	i shtrenjtë	[i ʃtréɲtə]
It's expensive	Është e shtrenjtë	[əʃtə ɛ ʃtréɲtə]

hire (n)	qiramarrje (f)	[ciramárjɛ]
to hire (~ a dinner jacket)	marr me qira	[mar mɛ cirá]
credit (trade credit)	kredit (m)	[krɛdít]
on credit (adv)	me kredi	[mɛ krɛdí]

CLOTHING & ACCESSORIES

32. Outerwear. Coats

clothes	**rroba** (f)	[róba]
outerwear	**veshje e sipërme** (f)	[véʃjɛ ɛ sípərmɛ]
winter clothing	**veshje dimri** (f)	[véʃjɛ dímri]
coat (overcoat)	**pallto** (f)	[páɫto]
fur coat	**gëzof** (m)	[gəzófʃ]
fur jacket	**xhaketë lëkure** (f)	[dʒakétə ləkúrɛ]
down coat	**xhup** (m)	[dʒup]
jacket (e.g. leather ~)	**xhaketë** (f)	[dʒakétə]
raincoat (trenchcoat, etc.)	**pardesy** (f)	[pardɛsý]
waterproof (adj)	**kundër shiut**	[kúndər ʃiut]

33. Men's & women's clothing

shirt (button shirt)	**këmishë** (f)	[kəmíʃə]
trousers	**pantallona** (f)	[pantaɫóna]
jeans	**xhinse** (f)	[dʒínsɛ]
suit jacket	**xhaketë kostumi** (f)	[dʒakétə kostúmi]
suit	**kostum** (m)	[kostúm]
dress (frock)	**fustan** (m)	[fustán]
skirt	**fund** (m)	[fund]
blouse	**bluzë** (f)	[blúzə]
knitted jacket (cardigan, etc.)	**xhaketë me thurje** (f)	[dʒakétə mɛ θúrjɛ]
jacket (of a woman's suit)	**xhaketë femrash** (f)	[dʒakétə fémraʃ]
T-shirt	**bluzë** (f)	[blúzə]
shorts (short trousers)	**pantallona të shkurtra** (f)	[pantaɫóna tə ʃkúrtra]
tracksuit	**tuta sportive** (f)	[túta sportívɛ]
bathrobe	**peshqir trupi** (m)	[pɛʃcír trúpi]
pyjamas	**pizhame** (f)	[piʒámɛ]
jumper (sweater)	**triko** (f)	[tríko]
pullover	**pulovër** (m)	[pulóvər]
waistcoat	**jelek** (m)	[jɛlék]
tailcoat	**frak** (m)	[frak]
dinner suit	**smoking** (m)	[smokíŋ]
uniform	**uniformë** (f)	[unifórmə]
workwear	**rroba pune** (f)	[róba púnɛ]
boiler suit	**kominoshe** (f)	[kominóʃɛ]
coat (e.g. doctor's smock)	**uniformë** (f)	[unifórmə]

34. Clothing. Underwear

underwear	të brendshme (f)	[tə bréndʃmɛ]
pants	boksera (f)	[bokséra]
panties	brekë (f)	[brékə]
vest (singlet)	fanellë (f)	[fanéɫə]
socks	çorape (pl)	[tʃorápɛ]
nightdress	këmishë nate (f)	[kəmíʃə nátɛ]
bra	sytjena (f)	[sytjéna]
knee highs (knee-high socks)	çorape déri tek gjuri (pl)	[tʃorápɛ déri ték ɟúri]
tights	geta (f)	[géta]
stockings (hold ups)	çorape të holla (pl)	[tʃorápɛ tə hóɫa]
swimsuit, bikini	rrobë banje (f)	[róbə báɲɛ]

35. Headwear

hat	kapelë (f)	[kapélə]
trilby hat	kapelë republike (f)	[kapélə rɛpublíkɛ]
baseball cap	kapelë bejsbolli (f)	[kapélə bɛjsbóɫi]
flatcap	kapelë e sheshtë (f)	[kapélə ɛ ʃéʃtə]
beret	beretë (f)	[bɛrétə]
hood	kapuç (m)	[kapútʃ]
panama hat	kapelë panama (f)	[kapélə panamá]
knit cap (knitted hat)	kapuç leshi (m)	[kapútʃ léʃi]
headscarf	shami (f)	[ʃamí]
women's hat	kapelë femrash (f)	[kapélə fémraʃ]
hard hat	helmetë (f)	[hɛlmétə]
forage cap	kapelë ushtrie (f)	[kapélə uʃtríɛ]
helmet	helmetë (f)	[hɛlmétə]
bowler	kapelë derby (f)	[kapélə dérby]
top hat	kapelë cilindër (f)	[kapélə tsilíndər]

36. Footwear

footwear	këpucë (pl)	[kəpútsə]
shoes (men's shoes)	këpucë burrash (pl)	[kəpútsə búraʃ]
shoes (women's shoes)	këpucë grash (pl)	[kəpútsə gráʃ]
boots (e.g., cowboy ~)	çizme (pl)	[tʃízmɛ]
carpet slippers	pantofla (pl)	[pantófla]
trainers	atlete tenisi (pl)	[atlétɛ tɛnísi]
trainers	atlete (pl)	[atlétɛ]
sandals	sandale (pl)	[sandálɛ]
cobbler (shoe repairer)	këpucëtar (m)	[kəputsətár]
heel	takë (f)	[tákə]

pair (of shoes)	palë (f)	[pálə]
lace (shoelace)	lidhëse këpucësh (f)	[líðəsɛ kəpútsəʃ]
to lace up (vt)	lidh këpucët	[lið kəpútsət]
shoehorn	lugë këpucësh (f)	[lúgə kəpútsəʃ]
shoe polish	bojë këpucësh (f)	[bójə kəpútsəʃ]

37. Personal accessories

gloves	dorëza (pl)	[dórəza]
mittens	doreza (f)	[doréza]
scarf (muffler)	shall (m)	[ʃaɫ]

glasses	syze (f)	[sýzɛ]
frame (eyeglass ~)	skelet syzesh (m)	[skɛlét sýzɛʃ]
umbrella	çadër (f)	[tʃádər]
walking stick	bastun (m)	[bastún]
hairbrush	furçë flokësh (f)	[fúrtʃə flókəʃ]
fan	erashkë (f)	[ɛráʃkə]

tie (necktie)	kravatë (f)	[kravátə]
bow tie	papion (m)	[papión]
braces	aski (pl)	[askí]
handkerchief	shami (f)	[ʃamí]

comb	krehër (m)	[kréhər]
hair slide	kapëse flokësh (f)	[kápəsɛ flókəʃ]
hairpin	karficë (f)	[karfítsə]
buckle	tokëz (f)	[tókəz]

belt	rrip (m)	[rip]
shoulder strap	rrip supi (m)	[rip súpi]

bag (handbag)	çantë dore (f)	[tʃántə dórɛ]
handbag	çantë (f)	[tʃántə]
rucksack	çantë shpine (f)	[tʃántə ʃpínɛ]

38. Clothing. Miscellaneous

fashion	modë (f)	[módə]
in vogue (adj)	në modë	[nə módə]
fashion designer	stilist (m)	[stilíst]

collar	jakë (f)	[jákə]
pocket	xhep (m)	[dʒɛp]
pocket (as adj)	i xhepit	[i dʒépit]
sleeve	mëngë (f)	[mə́ŋə]
hanging loop	hallkë për varje (f)	[háɫkə pər várjɛ]
flies (on trousers)	zinxhir (m)	[zindʒír]

zip (fastener)	zinxhir (m)	[zindʒír]
fastener	kapëse (f)	[kápəsɛ]
button	kopsë (f)	[kópsə]

| buttonhole | vrimë kopse (f) | [vrímə kópsɛ] |
| to come off (ab. button) | këputet | [kəpútɛt] |

to sew (vi, vt)	qep	[cɛp]
to embroider (vi, vt)	qëndis	[cəndís]
embroidery	qëndisje (f)	[cəndísjɛ]
sewing needle	gjilpërë për qepje (f)	[ɟilpérə pər cépjɛ]
thread	pe (m)	[pɛ]
seam	tegel (m)	[tɛgél]

to get dirty (vi)	bëhem pis	[béhɛm pis]
stain (mark, spot)	njollë (f)	[ɲótə]
to crease, to crumple	zhubros	[ʒubrós]
to tear, to rip (vt)	gris	[gris]
clothes moth	molë rrobash (f)	[mólə róbaʃ]

39. Personal care. Cosmetics

toothpaste	pastë dhëmbësh (f)	[pástə ðémbəʃ]
toothbrush	furçë dhëmbësh (f)	[fúrtʃə ðémbəʃ]
to clean one's teeth	laj dhëmbët	[laj ðémbət]

razor	brisk (m)	[brísk]
shaving cream	pastë rroje (f)	[pástə rójɛ]
to shave (vi)	rruhem	[rúhɛm]

| soap | sapun (m) | [sapún] |
| shampoo | shampo (f) | [ʃampó] |

scissors	gërshërë (f)	[gərʃérə]
nail file	limë thonjsh (f)	[límə θóɲʃ]
nail clippers	prerëse thonjsh (f)	[prérəsɛ θóɲʃ]
tweezers	piskatore vetullash (f)	[piskatórɛ vétutaʃ]

cosmetics	kozmetikë (f)	[kozmɛtíkə]
face mask	maskë fytyre (f)	[máskə fytýrɛ]
manicure	manikyr (m)	[manikýr]
to have a manicure	bëj manikyr	[bəj manikýr]
pedicure	pedikyr (m)	[pɛdikýr]

make-up bag	çantë kozmetike (f)	[tʃántə kozmɛtíkɛ]
face powder	pudër fytyre (f)	[púdər fytýrɛ]
powder compact	pudër kompakte (f)	[púdər kompáktɛ]
blusher	ruzh (m)	[ruʒ]

perfume (bottled)	parfum (m)	[parfúm]
toilet water (lotion)	parfum (m)	[parfúm]
lotion	krem (m)	[krɛm]
cologne	kolonjë (f)	[kolóɲə]

eyeshadow	rimel (m)	[rimél]
eyeliner	laps për sy (m)	[láps pər sy]
mascara	rimel (m)	[rimél]
lipstick	buzëkuq (m)	[buzəkúc]

nail polish	llak për thonj (m)	[ɬak pər θóɲ]
hair spray	llak flokësh (m)	[ɬak flókəʃ]
deodorant	deodorant (m)	[dɛodoránt]

cream	krem (m)	[krɛm]
face cream	krem për fytyrë (m)	[krɛm pər fytýrə]
hand cream	krem për duar (m)	[krɛm pər dúar]
anti-wrinkle cream	krem kundër rrudhave (m)	[krɛm kúndər rúðavɛ]
day cream	krem dite (m)	[krɛm dítɛ]
night cream	krem nate (m)	[krɛm nátɛ]
day (as adj)	dite	[dítɛ]
night (as adj)	nate	[nátɛ]

tampon	tampon (m)	[tampón]
toilet paper (toilet roll)	letër higjienike (f)	[létər hiɟiɛníkɛ]
hair dryer	tharëse flokësh (f)	[θárəsɛ flókəʃ]

40. Watches. Clocks

watch (wristwatch)	orë dore (f)	[órə dórɛ]
dial	faqe e orës (f)	[fácɛ ɛ órəs]
hand (clock, watch)	akrep (m)	[akrép]
metal bracelet	rrip metalik ore (m)	[rip mɛtalík órɛ]
watch strap	rrip ore (m)	[rip órɛ]

battery	bateri (f)	[batɛrí]
to be flat (battery)	e shkarkuar	[ɛ ʃkarkúar]
to change a battery	ndërroj baterinë	[ndərój batɛrínə]
to run fast	kalon shpejt	[kalón ʃpéjt]
to run slow	ngel prapa	[ŋɛl prápa]

wall clock	orë muri (f)	[órə múri]
hourglass	orë rëre (f)	[órə rərɛ]
sundial	orë diellore (f)	[órə diɛtórɛ]
alarm clock	orë me zile (f)	[órə mɛ zílɛ]
watchmaker	orëndreqës (m)	[orəndrécəs]
to repair (vt)	ndreq	[ndréc]

EVERYDAY EXPERIENCE

41. Money

money	para (f)	[pará]
currency exchange	këmbim valutor (m)	[kəmbím valutór]
exchange rate	kurs këmbimi (m)	[kurs kəmbími]
cashpoint	bankomat (m)	[bankomát]
coin	monedhë (f)	[monéðə]

dollar	dollar (m)	[doɫár]
euro	euro (f)	[éuro]

lira	lirë (f)	[lírə]
Deutschmark	Marka gjermane (f)	[márka ɟermánɛ]
franc	franga (f)	[fráŋa]
pound sterling	sterlina angleze (f)	[stɛrlína aŋlézɛ]
yen	jen (m)	[jén]

debt	borxh (m)	[bórdʒ]
debtor	debitor (m)	[dɛbitór]
to lend (money)	jap hua	[jap huá]
to borrow (vi, vt)	marr hua	[mar huá]

bank	bankë (f)	[bánkə]
account	llogari (f)	[ɫogarí]
to deposit (vt)	depozitoj	[dɛpozitój]
to deposit into the account	depozitoj në llogari	[dɛpozitój nə ɫogarí]
to withdraw (vt)	tërheq	[tərhéc]

credit card	kartë krediti (f)	[kártə krɛdíti]
cash	kesh (m)	[kɛʃ]
cheque	çek (m)	[tʃɛk]
to write a cheque	lëshoj një çek	[ləʃój ɲə tʃék]
chequebook	bllok çeqesh (m)	[bɫók tʃécɛʃ]

wallet	portofol (m)	[portofól]
purse	kuletë (f)	[kulétə]
safe	kasafortë (f)	[kasafórtə]

heir	trashëgimtar (m)	[traʃəgimtár]
inheritance	trashëgimi (f)	[traʃəgimí]
fortune (wealth)	pasuri (f)	[pasurí]

lease	qira (f)	[cirá]
rent (money)	qiraja (f)	[cirája]
to rent (sth from sb)	marr me qira	[mar mɛ cirá]

price	çmim (m)	[tʃmím]
cost	kosto (f)	[kósto]

sum	shumë (f)	[ʃúmə]
to spend (vt)	shpenzoj	[ʃpɛnzój]
expenses	shpenzime (f)	[ʃpɛnzímɛ]
to economize (vi, vt)	kursej	[kuɾséj]
economical	ekonomik	[ɛkonomík]

to pay (vi, vt)	paguaj	[pagúaj]
payment	pagesë (f)	[pagésə]
change (give the ~)	kusur (m)	[kusúɾ]

tax	taksë (f)	[táksə]
fine	gjobë (f)	[ɟóbə]
to fine (vt)	vendos gjobë	[vɛndós ɟóbə]

42. Post. Postal service

post office	zyrë postare (f)	[zýɾə postáɾɛ]
post (letters, etc.)	postë (f)	[póstə]
postman	postier (m)	[postiéɾ]
opening hours	orari i punës (m)	[oɾári i púnəs]

letter	letër (f)	[létəɾ]
registered letter	letër rekomande (f)	[létəɾ ɾɛkomándɛ]
postcard	kartolinë (f)	[kartolínə]
telegram	telegram (m)	[tɛlɛgrám]
parcel	pako (f)	[páko]
money transfer	transfer parash (m)	[transféɾ paráʃ]

to receive (vt)	pranoj	[pranój]
to send (vt)	dërgoj	[dərgój]
sending	dërgesë (f)	[dərgésə]
address	adresë (f)	[adrésə]
postcode	kodi postar (m)	[kódi postáɾ]
sender	dërguesi (m)	[dərgúɛsi]
receiver	pranues (m)	[pranúɛs]

name (first name)	emër (m)	[émər]
surname (last name)	mbiemër (m)	[mbiémər]
postage rate	tarifë postare (f)	[taɾífə postáɾɛ]
standard (adj)	standard	[standárd]
economical (adj)	ekonomike	[ɛkonomíkɛ]

weight	peshë (f)	[péʃə]
to weigh (~ letters)	peshoj	[pɛʃój]
envelope	zarf (m)	[zarf]
postage stamp	pullë postare (f)	[púɫə postáɾɛ]
to stamp an envelope	vendos pullën postare	[vɛndós púɫən postáɾɛ]

43. Banking

| bank | bankë (f) | [bánkə] |
| branch (of a bank) | degë (f) | [dégə] |

| consultant | punonjës banke (m) | [punóɲəs bánkɛ] |
| manager (director) | drejtor (m) | [drɛjtór] |

bank account	llogari bankare (f)	[ɫogarí bankárɛ]
account number	numër llogarie (m)	[númər ɫogaríɛ]
current account	llogari rrjedhëse (f)	[ɫogarí rjéðəsɛ]
deposit account	llogari kursimesh (f)	[ɫogarí kursímɛʃ]

to open an account	hap një llogari	[hap ɲə ɫogarí]
to close the account	mbyll një llogari	[mbýɫ ɲə ɫogarí]
to deposit into the account	depozitoj në llogari	[dɛpozitój nə ɫogarí]
to withdraw (vt)	tërheq	[tərhéc]

deposit	depozitë (f)	[dɛpozítə]
to make a deposit	kryej një depozitim	[krýɛj ɲə dɛpozitím]
wire transfer	transfer bankar (m)	[transfér bankár]
to wire, to transfer	transferoj para	[transfɛrój pará]

| sum | shumë (f) | [ʃúmə] |
| How much? | Sa? | [sa?] |

| signature | nënshkrim (m) | [nənʃkrím] |
| to sign (vt) | nënshkruaj | [nənʃkrúaj] |

credit card	kartë krediti (f)	[kártə krɛdíti]
code (PIN code)	kodi PIN (m)	[kódi pin]
credit card number	numri i kartës së kreditit (m)	[númri i kártəs sə krɛdítit]
cashpoint	bankomat (m)	[bankomát]

cheque	çek (m)	[tʃɛk]
to write a cheque	lëshoj një çek	[ləʃój ɲə tʃék]
chequebook	bllok çeqesh (m)	[bɫók tʃécɛʃ]

loan (bank ~)	kredi (f)	[krɛdí]
to apply for a loan	aplikoj për kredi	[aplikój pər krɛdí]
to get a loan	marr kredi	[mar krɛdí]
to give a loan	jap kredi	[jap krɛdí]
guarantee	garanci (f)	[garantsí]

44. Telephone. Phone conversation

telephone	telefon (m)	[tɛlɛfón]
mobile phone	celular (m)	[tsɛlulár]
answerphone	sekretari telefonike (f)	[sɛkrɛtarí tɛlɛfoníkɛ]

| to call (by phone) | telefonoj | [tɛlɛfonój] |
| call, ring | telefonatë (f) | [tɛlɛfonátə] |

to dial a number	i bie numrit	[i bíɛ númrit]
Hello!	Përshëndetje!	[pərʃəndétjɛ!]
to ask (vt)	pyes	[pýɛs]
to answer (vi, vt)	përgjigjem	[pərɟíɟɛm]
to hear (vt)	dëgjoj	[dəɟój]
well (adv)	mirë	[mírə]

| not well (adv) | jo mirë | [jo mírə] |
| noises (interference) | zhurmë (f) | [ʒúrmə] |

receiver	marrës (m)	[márəs]
to pick up (~ the phone)	ngre telefonin	[ŋré tɛlɛfónin]
to hang up (~ the phone)	mbyll telefonin	[mbýɫ tɛlɛfónin]

busy (engaged)	i zënë	[i zénə]
to ring (ab. phone)	bie zilja	[bíɛ zílja]
telephone book	numerator telefonik (m)	[numɛratór tɛlɛfoník]

local (adj)	lokale	[lokálɛ]
local call	thirrje lokale (f)	[θírjɛ lokálɛ]
trunk (e.g. ~ call)	distancë e largët	[distántsə ɛ lárgət]
trunk call	thirrje në distancë (f)	[θírjɛ nə distántsə]
international (adj)	ndërkombëtar	[ndərkombətár]
international call	thirrje ndërkombëtare (f)	[θírjɛ ndərkombətárɛ]

45. Mobile telephone

mobile phone	celular (m)	[tsɛlulár]
display	ekran (m)	[ɛkrán]
button	buton (m)	[butón]
SIM card	karta SIM (m)	[kárta sim]

battery	bateri (f)	[batɛrí]
to be flat (battery)	e shkarkuar	[ɛ ʃkarkúar]
charger	karikues (m)	[karikúɛs]

menu	menu (f)	[mɛnú]
settings	parametra (f)	[paramétra]
tune (melody)	melodi (f)	[mɛlodí]
to select (vt)	përzgjedh	[pərzɟéð]

calculator	makinë llogaritëse (f)	[makínə ɫogarítəsɛ]
voice mail	postë zanore (f)	[póstə zanórɛ]
alarm clock	alarm (m)	[alárm]
contacts	kontakte (pl)	[kontáktɛ]

| SMS (text message) | SMS (m) | [ɛsɛmɛs] |
| subscriber | abonent (m) | [abonént] |

46. Stationery

| ballpoint pen | stilolaps (m) | [stiloláps] |
| fountain pen | stilograf (m) | [stilográf] |

pencil	laps (m)	[láps]
highlighter	shënjues (m)	[ʃəɲúɛs]
felt-tip pen	tushë me bojë (f)	[túʃə mɛ bójə]
notepad	bllok shënimesh (m)	[bɫók ʃənímɛʃ]
diary	agjendë (f)	[aɟéndə]

ruler	vizore (f)	[vizórɛ]
calculator	makinë llogaritëse (f)	[makínə ɫogarítəsɛ]
rubber	gomë (f)	[gómə]
drawing pin	pineskë (f)	[pinéskə]
paper clip	kapëse fletësh (f)	[kápəsɛ flétəʃ]

glue	ngjitës (m)	[ɲʝítəs]
stapler	ngjitës metalik (m)	[ɲʝítəs mɛtalík]
hole punch	hapës vrimash (m)	[hápəs vrímaʃ]
pencil sharpener	mprehëse lapsash (m)	[mpréhəsɛ lápsaʃ]

47. Foreign languages

language	gjuhë (f)	[ʝúhə]
foreign (adj)	huaj	[húaj]
foreign language	gjuhë e huaj (f)	[ʝúhə ɛ húaj]
to study (vt)	studioj	[studiój]
to learn (language, etc.)	mësoj	[məsój]

to read (vi, vt)	lexoj	[lɛdzój]
to speak (vi, vt)	flas	[flas]
to understand (vt)	kuptoj	[kuptój]
to write (vt)	shkruaj	[ʃkrúaj]

fast (adv)	shpejt	[ʃpɛjt]
slowly (adv)	ngadalë	[ŋadálə]
fluently (adv)	rrjedhshëm	[rrjéðʃəm]

rules	rregullat (pl)	[réguɫat]
grammar	gramatikë (f)	[gramatíkə]
vocabulary	fjalor (m)	[fjalór]
phonetics	fonetikë (f)	[fonɛtíkə]

textbook	tekst mësimor (m)	[tɛkst məsimór]
dictionary	fjalor (m)	[fjalór]
teach-yourself book	libër i mësimit autodidakt (m)	[líbər i məsímit autodidákt]
phrasebook	libër frazeologjik (m)	[líbər frazɛoloʝík]

cassette, tape	kasetë (f)	[kasétə]
videotape	videokasetë (f)	[vidɛokasétə]
CD, compact disc	CD (f)	[tsɛdé]
DVD	DVD (m)	[dividí]

alphabet	alfabet (m)	[alfabét]
to spell (vt)	gërmëzoj	[gərməzój]
pronunciation	shqiptim (m)	[ʃciptím]

accent	aksent (m)	[aksént]
with an accent	me aksent	[mɛ aksént]
without an accent	pa aksent	[pa aksént]

| word | fjalë (f) | [fjálə] |
| meaning | kuptim (m) | [kuptím] |

course (e.g. a French ~)	**kurs** (m)	[kurs]
to sign up	**regjistrohem**	[rɛɟistróhɛm]
teacher	**mësues** (m)	[məsúɛs]

translation (process)	**përkthim** (m)	[pərkθím]
translation (text, etc.)	**përkthim** (m)	[pərkθím]
translator	**përkthyes** (m)	[pərkθýɛs]
interpreter	**përkthyes** (m)	[pərkθýɛs]

polyglot	**poliglot** (m)	[poliglót]
memory	**kujtesë** (f)	[kujtésə]

MEALS. RESTAURANT

48. Table setting

spoon	lugë (f)	[lúgə]
knife	thikë (f)	[θíkə]
fork	pirun (m)	[pirún]
cup (e.g., coffee ~)	filxhan (m)	[fildʒán]
plate (dinner ~)	pjatë (f)	[pjátə]
saucer	pjatë filxhani (f)	[pjátə fildʒáni]
serviette	pecetë (f)	[pɛtsétə]
toothpick	kruajtëse dhëmbësh (f)	[krúajtəsɛ ðə́mbəʃ]

49. Restaurant

restaurant	restorant (m)	[rɛstoránt]
coffee bar	kafene (f)	[kafɛné]
pub, bar	pab (m), pijetore (f)	[pab], [pijɛtórɛ]
tearoom	çajtore (f)	[tʃajtórɛ]
waiter	kamerier (m)	[kamɛriér]
waitress	kameriere (f)	[kamɛriérɛ]
barman	banakier (m)	[banakiér]
menu	menu (f)	[mɛnú]
wine list	menu verërash (f)	[mɛnú vérəraʃ]
to book a table	rezervoj një tavolinë	[rɛzɛrvój ɲə tavolínə]
course, dish	pjatë (f)	[pjátə]
to order (meal)	porosis	[porosís]
to make an order	bëj porosinë	[bəj porosínə]
aperitif	aperitiv (m)	[apɛritív]
starter	antipastë (f)	[antipástə]
dessert, pudding	ëmbëlsirë (f)	[əmbəlsírə]
bill	faturë (f)	[fatúrə]
to pay the bill	paguaj faturën	[pagúaj fatúrən]
to give change	jap kusur	[jap kusúr]
tip	bakshish (m)	[bakʃíʃ]

50. Meals

food	ushqim (m)	[uʃcím]
to eat (vi, vt)	ha	[ha]

breakfast	mëngjes (m)	[mənɟés]
to have breakfast	ha mëngjes	[ha mənɟés]
lunch	drekë (f)	[drékə]
to have lunch	ha drekë	[ha drékə]
dinner	darkë (f)	[dárkə]
to have dinner	ha darkë	[ha dárkə]

| appetite | oreks (m) | [oréks] |
| Enjoy your meal! | Të bëftë mirë! | [tə bəftə mírə!] |

to open (~ a bottle)	hap	[hap]
to spill (liquid)	derdh	[dérð]
to spill out (vi)	derdhje	[dérðjɛ]

to boil (vi)	ziej	[zíɛj]
to boil (vt)	ziej	[zíɛj]
boiled (~ water)	i zier	[i zíɛr]
to chill, cool down (vt)	ftoh	[ftoh]
to chill (vi)	ftohje	[ftóhjɛ]

| taste, flavour | shije (f) | [ʃíjɛ] |
| aftertaste | shije (f) | [ʃíjɛ] |

to slim down (lose weight)	dobësohem	[dobəsóhɛm]
diet	dietë (f)	[diétə]
vitamin	vitaminë (f)	[vitamínə]
calorie	kalori (f)	[kalorí]
vegetarian (n)	vegjetarian (m)	[vɛɟɛtarián]
vegetarian (adj)	vegjetarian	[vɛɟɛtarián]

fats (nutrient)	yndyrë (f)	[yndýrə]
proteins	proteinë (f)	[protɛínə]
carbohydrates	karbohidrat (m)	[karbohidrát]

slice (of lemon, ham)	fetë (f)	[fétə]
piece (of cake, pie)	copë (f)	[tsópə]
crumb (of bread, cake, etc.)	dromcë (f)	[drómtsə]

51. Cooked dishes

course, dish	pjatë (f)	[pjátə]
cuisine	kuzhinë (f)	[kuʒínə]
recipe	recetë (f)	[rɛtsétə]
portion	racion (m)	[ratsión]

| salad | sallatë (f) | [saɬátə] |
| soup | supë (f) | [súpə] |

clear soup (broth)	lëng mishi (m)	[ləŋ míʃi]
sandwich (bread)	sandviç (m)	[sandvítʃ]
fried eggs	vezë të skuqura (pl)	[vézə tə skúcura]

| hamburger (beefburger) | hamburger | [hamburgér] |
| beefsteak | biftek (m) | [bifték] |

side dish	garniturë (f)	[garnitúrə]
spaghetti	shpageti (pl)	[ʃpagéti]
mash	pure patatesh (f)	[puré patátɛʃ]
pizza	pica (f)	[pítsa]
porridge (oatmeal, etc.)	qull (m)	[cuɫ]
omelette	omëletë (f)	[oməlétə]

boiled (e.g. ~ beef)	i zier	[i zíɛr]
smoked (adj)	i tymosur	[i tymósur]
fried (adj)	i skuqur	[i skúcur]
dried (adj)	i tharë	[i θárə]
frozen (adj)	i ngrirë	[i ŋrírə]
pickled (adj)	i marinuar	[i marinúar]

sweet (sugary)	i ëmbël	[i émbəl]
salty (adj)	i kripur	[i krípur]
cold (adj)	i ftohtë	[i ftóhtə]
hot (adj)	i nxehtë	[i ndzéhtə]
bitter (adj)	i hidhur	[i híður]
tasty (adj)	i shijshëm	[i ʃíʃəm]

to cook in boiling water	ziej	[zíɛj]
to cook (dinner)	gatuaj	[gatúaj]
to fry (vt)	skuq	[skuc]
to heat up (food)	ngroh	[ŋróh]

to salt (vt)	hedh kripë	[hɛð krípə]
to pepper (vt)	hedh piper	[hɛð pipér]
to grate (vt)	rendoj	[rɛndój]
peel (n)	lëkurë (f)	[ləkúrə]
to peel (vt)	qëroj	[cərój]

52. Food

meat	mish (m)	[miʃ]
chicken	pulë (f)	[púlə]
poussin	mish pule (m)	[miʃ púlɛ]
duck	rosë (f)	[rósə]
goose	patë (f)	[pátə]
game	gjah (m)	[ɟáh]
turkey	mish gjel deti (m)	[miʃ ɟɛl déti]

pork	mish derri (m)	[miʃ déri]
veal	mish viçi (m)	[miʃ vítʃi]
lamb	mish qengji (m)	[miʃ cénɟi]
beef	mish lope (m)	[miʃ lópɛ]
rabbit	mish lepuri (m)	[miʃ lépuri]

sausage (bologna, etc.)	salsiçe (f)	[salsítʃɛ]
vienna sausage (frankfurter)	salsiçe vjeneze (f)	[salsítʃɛ vjɛnézɛ]
bacon	proshutë (f)	[proʃútə]
ham	sallam (m)	[saɫám]
gammon	kofshë derri (f)	[kófʃə déri]
pâté	pate (f)	[paté]

liver	mëlçi (f)	[məltʃí]
mince (minced meat)	hamburger (m)	[hamburgér]
tongue	gjuhë (f)	[ɟúhə]

egg	ve (f)	[vɛ]
eggs	vezë (pl)	[vézə]
egg white	e bardhë veze (f)	[ɛ bárðə vézɛ]
egg yolk	e verdhë veze (f)	[ɛ vérðə vézɛ]

fish	peshk (m)	[pɛʃk]
seafood	fruta deti (pl)	[frúta déti]
crustaceans	krustace (pl)	[krustátsɛ]
caviar	havjar (m)	[havjár]

crab	gaforre (f)	[gafórɛ]
prawn	karkalec (m)	[karkaléts]
oyster	midhje (f)	[míðjɛ]
spiny lobster	karavidhe (f)	[karavíðɛ]
octopus	oktapod (m)	[oktapód]
squid	kallamarë (f)	[kałamárə]

sturgeon	bli (m)	[blí]
salmon	salmon (m)	[salmón]
halibut	shojzë e Atlantikut Verior (f)	[ʃójzə ɛ atlantíkut vɛriór]

cod	merluc (m)	[mɛrlúts]
mackerel	skumbri (m)	[skúmbri]
tuna	tunë (f)	[túnə]
eel	ngjalë (f)	[nɟálə]

trout	troftë (f)	[tróftə]
sardine	sardele (f)	[sardélɛ]
pike	mlysh (m)	[mlýʃ]
herring	harengë (f)	[haréŋə]

bread	bukë (f)	[búkə]
cheese	djath (m)	[djáθ]
sugar	sheqer (m)	[ʃɛcér]
salt	kripë (f)	[krípə]

rice	oriz (m)	[oríz]
pasta (macaroni)	makarona (f)	[makaróna]
noodles	makarona petë (f)	[makaróna pétə]

butter	gjalp (m)	[ɟalp]
vegetable oil	vaj vegjetal (m)	[vaj vɛɟɛtál]
sunflower oil	vaj luledielli (m)	[vaj lulɛdiéti]
margarine	margarinë (f)	[margarínə]

| olives | ullinj (pl) | [utíɲ] |
| olive oil | vaj ulliri (m) | [vaj utíri] |

milk	qumësht (m)	[cúməʃt]
condensed milk	qumësht i kondensuar (m)	[cúməʃt i kondɛnsúar]
yogurt	kos (m)	[kos]
soured cream	salcë kosi (f)	[sáltsə kosi]

cream (of milk)	krem qumështi (m)	[krɛm cúməʃti]
mayonnaise	majonezë (f)	[majonézə]
buttercream	krem gjalpi (m)	[krɛm ɟálpi]

groats (barley ~, etc.)	drithëra (pl)	[dríθəra]
flour	miell (m)	[míɛɫ]
tinned food	konserva (f)	[konsérva]

cornflakes	kornfleiks (m)	[kornfléiks]
honey	mjaltë (f)	[mjáltə]
jam	reçel (m)	[rɛtʃél]
chewing gum	çamçakëz (m)	[tʃamtʃakéz]

53. Drinks

water	ujë (m)	[újə]
drinking water	ujë i pijshëm (m)	[újə i píjʃəm]
mineral water	ujë mineral (m)	[újə minɛrál]

still (adj)	ujë natyral	[újə natyrál]
carbonated (adj)	ujë i karbonuar	[újə i karbonúar]
sparkling (adj)	ujë i gazuar	[újə i gazúar]
ice	akull (m)	[ákuɫ]
with ice	me akull	[mɛ ákuɫ]

non-alcoholic (adj)	jo alkoolik	[jo alkoolík]
soft drink	pije e lehtë (f)	[píjɛ ɛ léhtə]
refreshing drink	pije freskuese (f)	[píjɛ frɛskúɛsɛ]
lemonade	limonadë (f)	[limonádə]

spirits	likere (pl)	[likérɛ]
wine	verë (f)	[vérə]
white wine	verë e bardhë (f)	[vérə ɛ bárðə]
red wine	verë e kuqe (f)	[vérə ɛ kúcɛ]

liqueur	liker (m)	[likér]
champagne	shampanjë (f)	[ʃampáɲə]
vermouth	vermut (m)	[vɛrmút]

whisky	uiski (m)	[víski]
vodka	vodkë (f)	[vódkə]
gin	xhin (m)	[dʒin]
cognac	konjak (m)	[koɲák]
rum	rum (m)	[rum]

coffee	kafe (f)	[káfɛ]
black coffee	kafe e zezë (f)	[káfɛ ɛ zézə]
white coffee	kafe me qumësht (m)	[káfɛ mɛ cúməʃt]
cappuccino	kapuçino (m)	[kaputʃíno]
instant coffee	neskafe (f)	[nɛskáfɛ]

milk	qumësht (m)	[cúməʃt]
cocktail	koktej (m)	[koktéj]
milkshake	milkshake (f)	[milkʃákɛ]

juice	lëng frutash (m)	[lən frútaʃ]
tomato juice	lëng domatesh (m)	[lən domátɛʃ]
orange juice	lëng portokalli (m)	[lən portokáłi]
freshly squeezed juice	lëng frutash i freskët (m)	[lən frútaʃ i fréskət]

beer	birrë (f)	[bírə]
lager	birrë e lehtë (f)	[bíra ɛ léhtə]
bitter	birrë e zezë (f)	[bíra ɛ zézə]

tea	çaj (m)	[tʃáj]
black tea	çaj i zi (m)	[tʃáj i zí]
green tea	çaj jeshil (m)	[tʃáj jɛʃíl]

54. Vegetables

| vegetables | perime (pl) | [pɛrímɛ] |
| greens | zarzavate (pl) | [zarzavátɛ] |

tomato	domate (f)	[domátɛ]
cucumber	kastravec (m)	[kastravéts]
carrot	karotë (f)	[karótə]
potato	patate (f)	[patátɛ]
onion	qepë (f)	[cépə]
garlic	hudhër (f)	[húðər]

cabbage	lakër (f)	[lákər]
cauliflower	lulelakër (f)	[lulɛlákər]
Brussels sprouts	lakër Brukseli (f)	[lákər brukséli]
broccoli	brokoli (m)	[brókoli]

beetroot	panxhar (m)	[pandʒár]
aubergine	patëllxhan (m)	[patəłdʒán]
courgette	kungulleshë (m)	[kuŋułéʃə]

| pumpkin | kungull (m) | [kúŋuł] |
| turnip | rrepë (f) | [répə] |

parsley	majdanoz (m)	[majdanóz]
dill	kopër (f)	[kópər]
lettuce	sallatë jeshile (f)	[sałátə jɛʃílɛ]
celery	selino (f)	[sɛlíno]

| asparagus | asparagus (m) | [asparágus] |
| spinach | spinaq (m) | [spinác] |

| pea | bizele (f) | [bizélɛ] |
| beans | fasule (f) | [fasúlɛ] |

| maize | misër (m) | [mísər] |
| kidney bean | groshë (f) | [gróʃə] |

sweet paper	spec (m)	[spɛts]
radish	rrepkë (f)	[répkə]
artichoke	angjinare (f)	[anɟinárɛ]

55. Fruits. Nuts

fruit	**frut** (m)	[frut]
apple	**mollë** (f)	[mótə]
pear	**dardhë** (f)	[dárðə]
lemon	**limon** (m)	[limón]
orange	**portokall** (m)	[portokáł]
strawberry (garden ~)	**luleshtrydhe** (f)	[luleʃtrýðɛ]
tangerine	**mandarinë** (f)	[mandarínə]
plum	**kumbull** (f)	[kúmbuł]
peach	**pjeshkë** (f)	[pjéʃkə]
apricot	**kajsi** (f)	[kajsí]
raspberry	**mjedër** (f)	[mjédər]
pineapple	**ananas** (m)	[ananás]
banana	**banane** (f)	[banánɛ]
watermelon	**shalqi** (m)	[ʃalcí]
grape	**rrush** (m)	[ruʃ]
sour cherry	**qershi vishnje** (f)	[cɛrʃí víʃɲɛ]
sweet cherry	**qershi** (f)	[cɛrʃí]
melon	**pjepër** (m)	[pjépər]
grapefruit	**grejpfrut** (m)	[grɛjpfrút]
avocado	**avokado** (f)	[avokádo]
papaya	**papaja** (f)	[papája]
mango	**mango** (f)	[máŋo]
pomegranate	**shegë** (f)	[ʃégə]
redcurrant	**kaliboba e kuqe** (f)	[kalibóba ɛ kúcɛ]
blackcurrant	**kaliboba e zezë** (f)	[kalibóba ɛ zézə]
gooseberry	**kulumbri** (f)	[kulumbrí]
bilberry	**boronicë** (f)	[boronítsə]
blackberry	**manaferra** (f)	[manaféra]
raisin	**rrush i thatë** (m)	[ruʃ i θátə]
fig	**fik** (m)	[fik]
date	**hurmë** (f)	[húrmə]
peanut	**kikirik** (m)	[kikirík]
almond	**bajame** (f)	[bajámɛ]
walnut	**arrë** (f)	[árə]
hazelnut	**lajthi** (f)	[lajθí]
coconut	**arrë kokosi** (f)	[árə kokósi]
pistachios	**fëstëk** (m)	[fəsték]

56. Bread. Sweets

bakers' confectionery (pastry)	**ëmbëlsira** (pl)	[əmbəlsíra]
bread	**bukë** (f)	[búkə]
biscuits	**biskota** (pl)	[biskóta]
chocolate (n)	**çokollatë** (f)	[tʃokołátə]
chocolate (as adj)	**prej çokollate**	[prɛj tʃokołátɛ]

candy (wrapped)	karamele (f)	[karamélɛ]
cake (e.g. cupcake)	kek (m)	[kék]
cake (e.g. birthday ~)	tortë (f)	[tórtə]

| pie (e.g. apple ~) | tortë (f) | [tórtə] |
| filling (for cake, pie) | mbushje (f) | [mbúʃjɛ] |

jam (whole fruit jam)	reçel (m)	[rɛtʃél]
marmalade	marmelatë (f)	[marmɛlátə]
wafers	vafera (pl)	[vaféra]
ice-cream	akullore (f)	[akuɫórɛ]
pudding (Christmas ~)	puding (m)	[pudíŋ]

57. Spices

salt	kripë (f)	[krípə]
salty (adj)	i kripur	[i krípur]
to salt (vt)	hedh kripë	[hɛð krípə]

black pepper	piper i zi (m)	[pipér i zi]
red pepper (milled ~)	piper i kuq (m)	[pipér i kuc]
mustard	mustardë (f)	[mustárdə]
horseradish	rrepë djegëse (f)	[répə djégəsɛ]

condiment	salcë (f)	[sáltsə]
spice	erëz (f)	[érəz]
sauce	salcë (f)	[sáltsə]
vinegar	uthull (f)	[úθuɫ]

anise	anisetë (f)	[anisétə]
basil	borzilok (m)	[borzilók]
cloves	karafil (m)	[karafíl]
ginger	xhenxhefil (m)	[dʒɛndʒɛfíl]
coriander	koriandër (m)	[koriándər]
cinnamon	kanellë (f)	[kanéɫə]

sesame	susam (m)	[susám]
bay leaf	gjeth dafine (m)	[ɟɛθ dafínɛ]
paprika	spec (m)	[spɛts]
caraway	kumin (m)	[kumín]
saffron	shafran (m)	[ʃafrán]

PERSONAL INFORMATION. FAMILY

name (first name)	emër (m)	[émər]
surname (last name)	mbiemër (m)	[mbiémər]
date of birth	datëlindje (f)	[datəlíndjɛ]
place of birth	vendlindje (f)	[vɛndlíndjɛ]
nationality	kombësi (f)	[kombəsí]
place of residence	vendbanim (m)	[vɛndbaním]
country	shtet (m)	[ʃtɛt]
profession (occupation)	profesion (m)	[profɛsión]
gender, sex	gjinia (f)	[ɟinía]
height	gjatësia (f)	[ɟatəsía]
weight	peshë (f)	[péʃə]

mother	nënë (f)	[nénə]
father	baba (f)	[babá]
son	bir (m)	[bir]
daughter	bijë (f)	[bíjə]
younger daughter	vajza e vogël (f)	[vájza ɛ vógəl]
younger son	djali i vogël (m)	[djáli i vógəl]
eldest daughter	vajza e madhe (f)	[vájza ɛ máðɛ]
eldest son	djali i vogël (m)	[djáli i vógəl]
brother	vëlla (m)	[vəɫá]
elder brother	vëllai i madh (m)	[vəɫái i mað]
younger brother	vëllai i vogël (m)	[vəɫai i vógəl]
sister	motër (f)	[mótər]
elder sister	motra e madhe (f)	[mótra ɛ máðɛ]
younger sister	motra e vogël (f)	[mótra ɛ vógəl]
cousin (masc.)	kushëri (m)	[kuʃərí]
cousin (fem.)	kushërirë (f)	[kuʃərírə]
mummy	mami (f)	[mámi]
dad, daddy	babi (m)	[bábi]
parents	prindër (pl)	[príndər]
child	fëmijë (f)	[fəmíjə]
children	fëmijë (pl)	[fəmíjə]
grandmother	gjyshe (f)	[ɟýʃɛ]
grandfather	gjysh (m)	[ɟyʃ]

grandson	nip (m)	[nip]
granddaughter	mbesë (f)	[mbésə]
grandchildren	nipër e mbesa (pl)	[nípər ɛ mbésa]

uncle	dajë (f)	[dájə]
aunt	teze (f)	[tézɛ]
nephew	nip (m)	[nip]
niece	mbesë (f)	[mbésə]

mother-in-law (wife's mother)	vjehrrë (f)	[vjéhrə]
father-in-law (husband's father)	vjehrri (m)	[vjéhri]
son-in-law (daughter's husband)	dhëndër (m)	[ðéndər]
stepmother	njerkë (f)	[ɲérkə]
stepfather	njerk (m)	[ɲérk]

infant	foshnjë (f)	[fóʃnə]
baby (infant)	fëmijë (f)	[fəmíjə]
little boy, kid	djalosh (m)	[djalóʃ]

wife	bashkëshorte (f)	[baʃkəʃórtɛ]
husband	bashkëshort (m)	[baʃkəʃórt]
spouse (husband)	bashkëshort (m)	[baʃkəʃórt]
spouse (wife)	bashkëshorte (f)	[baʃkəʃórtɛ]

married (masc.)	i martuar	[i martúar]
married (fem.)	e martuar	[ɛ martúar]
single (unmarried)	beqar	[bɛcár]
bachelor	beqar (m)	[bɛcár]
divorced (masc.)	i divorcuar	[i divortsúar]
widow	vejushë (f)	[vɛjúʃə]
widower	vejan (m)	[vɛján]

relative	kushëri (m)	[kuʃərí]
close relative	kushëri i afërt (m)	[kuʃərí i áfərt]
distant relative	kushëri i largët (m)	[kuʃərí i lárgət]
relatives	kushërinj (pl)	[kuʃəríɲ]

orphan (boy)	jetim (m)	[jɛtím]
orphan (girl)	jetime (f)	[jɛtímɛ]
guardian (of a minor)	kujdestar (m)	[kujdɛstár]
to adopt (a boy)	adoptoj	[adoptój]
to adopt (a girl)	adoptoj	[adoptój]

60. Friends. Colleagues

friend (masc.)	mik (m)	[mik]
friend (fem.)	mike (f)	[míkɛ]
friendship	miqësi (f)	[micəsí]
to be friends	të miqësohem	[tə micəsóhɛm]
pal (masc.)	shok (m)	[ʃok]
pal (fem.)	shoqe (f)	[ʃócɛ]

partner	**partner** (m)	[partnér]
chief (boss)	**shef** (m)	[ʃɛf]
superior (n)	**epror** (m)	[ɛprór]
owner, proprietor	**pronar** (m)	[pronár]
subordinate (n)	**vartës** (m)	[vártəs]
colleague	**koleg** (m)	[kolég]
acquaintance (person)	**i njohur** (m)	[i ɲóhur]
fellow traveller	**bashkudhëtar** (m)	[baʃkuðətár]
classmate	**shok klase** (m)	[ʃok klásɛ]
neighbour (masc.)	**komshi** (m)	[komʃí]
neighbour (fem.)	**komshike** (f)	[komʃíkɛ]
neighbours	**komshinj** (pl)	[komʃíɲ]

HUMAN BODY. MEDICINE

61. Head

head	kokë (f)	[kókə]
face	fytyrë (f)	[fytýrə]
nose	hundë (f)	[húndə]
mouth	gojë (f)	[gójə]

eye	sy (m)	[sy]
eyes	sytë	[sýtə]
pupil	bebëz (f)	[bébəz]
eyebrow	vetull (f)	[vétuɫ]
eyelash	qerpik (m)	[cɛrpík]
eyelid	qepallë (f)	[cɛpáɫə]

tongue	gjuhë (f)	[ɟúhə]
tooth	dhëmb (m)	[ðəmb]
lips	buzë (f)	[búzə]
cheekbones	mollëza (f)	[móɫəza]
gum	mishrat e dhëmbëve	[míʃrat ɛ ðəmbəvɛ]
palate	qiellzë (f)	[ciéɫzə]

nostrils	vrimat e hundës (pl)	[vrímat ɛ húndəs]
chin	mjekër (f)	[mjékər]
jaw	nofull (f)	[nófuɫ]
cheek	faqe (f)	[fácɛ]

forehead	ball (m)	[báɫ]
temple	tëmth (m)	[təmθ]
ear	vesh (m)	[vɛʃ]
back of the head	zverk (m)	[zvɛrk]
neck	qafë (f)	[cáfə]
throat	fyt (m)	[fyt]

hair	flokë (pl)	[flókə]
hairstyle	model flokësh (m)	[modél flókəʃ]
haircut	prerje flokësh (f)	[prérjɛ flókəʃ]
wig	paruke (f)	[parúkɛ]

moustache	mustaqe (f)	[mustácɛ]
beard	mjekër (f)	[mjékər]
to have (a beard, etc.)	lë mjekër	[lə mjékər]
plait	gërshet (m)	[gərʃét]
sideboards	baseta (f)	[baséta]

red-haired (adj)	flokëkuqe	[flokəkúcɛ]
grey (hair)	thinja	[θíɲa]
bald (adj)	qeros	[cɛrós]
bald patch	tullë (f)	[túɫə]

| ponytail | bishtalec (m) | [biʃtaléts] |
| fringe | balluke (f) | [baɫúkɛ] |

62. Human body

| hand | dorë (f) | [dórə] |
| arm | krah (m) | [krah] |

finger	gisht i dorës (m)	[gíʃt i dórəs]
toe	gisht i këmbës (m)	[gíʃt i kémbəs]
thumb	gishti i madh (m)	[gíʃti i máð]
little finger	gishti i vogël (m)	[gíʃti i vógəl]
nail	thua (f)	[θúa]

fist	grusht (m)	[grúʃt]
palm	pëllëmbë dore (f)	[pəɫémbə dórɛ]
wrist	kyç (m)	[kytʃ]
forearm	parakrah (m)	[parakráh]
elbow	bërryl (m)	[bərýl]
shoulder	shpatull (f)	[ʃpátuɫ]

leg	këmbë (f)	[kémbə]
foot	shputë (f)	[ʃpútə]
knee	gju (m)	[ɟú]
calf	pulpë (f)	[púlpə]
hip	ijë (f)	[íjə]
heel	thembër (f)	[θémbər]

body	trup (m)	[trup]
stomach	stomak (m)	[stomák]
chest	kraharor (m)	[kraharór]
breast	gjoks (m)	[ɟóks]
flank	krah (m)	[krah]
back	kurriz (m)	[kuríz]
lower back	fundshpina (f)	[fundʃpína]
waist	beli (m)	[béli]

navel (belly button)	kërthizë (f)	[kərθízə]
buttocks	vithe (f)	[víθɛ]
bottom	prapanica (f)	[prapanítsa]

beauty spot	nishan (m)	[niʃán]
birthmark (café au lait spot)	shenjë lindjeje (f)	[ʃéɲə líndjɛjɛ]
tattoo	tatuazh (m)	[tatuáʒ]
scar	shenjë (f)	[ʃéɲə]

63. Diseases

illness	sëmundje (f)	[səmúndjɛ]
to be ill	jam sëmurë	[jam səmúrə]
health	shëndet (m)	[ʃəndét]
runny nose (coryza)	rrifë (f)	[rífə]

tonsillitis	grykët (m)	[grýkət]
cold (illness)	ftohje (f)	[ftóhjɛ]
to catch a cold	ftohem	[ftóhɛm]

bronchitis	bronkit (m)	[bronkít]
pneumonia	pneumoni (f)	[pnɛumoní]
flu, influenza	grip (m)	[grip]

shortsighted (adj)	miop	[mióp]
longsighted (adj)	presbit	[prɛsbít]
strabismus (crossed eyes)	strabizëm (m)	[strabízəm]
squint-eyed (adj)	strabik	[strabík]
cataract	katarakt (m)	[katarákt]
glaucoma	glaukoma (f)	[glaukóma]

stroke	goditje (f)	[godítjɛ]
heart attack	sulm në zemër (m)	[sulm nə zémər]
myocardial infarction	infarkt miokardiak (m)	[infárkt miokardiák]
paralysis	paralizë (f)	[paralízə]
to paralyse (vt)	paralizoj	[paralizój]

allergy	alergji (f)	[alɛrɟí]
asthma	astmë (f)	[ástmə]
diabetes	diabet (m)	[diabét]

| toothache | dhimbje dhëmbi (f) | [ðímbjɛ ðə́mbi] |
| caries | karies (m) | [kariés] |

diarrhoea	diarre (f)	[diaré]
constipation	kapsllëk (m)	[kapsɫə́k]
stomach upset	dispepsi (f)	[dispɛpsí]
food poisoning	helmim (m)	[hɛlmím]
to get food poisoning	helmohem nga ushqimi	[hɛlmóhɛm ŋa uʃcími]

arthritis	artrit (m)	[artrít]
rickets	rakit (m)	[rakít]
rheumatism	reumatizëm (m)	[rɛumatízəm]
atherosclerosis	arteriosklerozë (f)	[artɛrioskɫɛrózə]

gastritis	gastrit (m)	[gastrít]
appendicitis	apendicit (m)	[apɛnditsít]
cholecystitis	kolecistit (m)	[kolɛtsistít]
ulcer	ulcerë (f)	[ultsérə]

measles	fruth (m)	[fruθ]
rubella (German measles)	rubeola (f)	[rubɛóla]
jaundice	verdhëza (f)	[vérðəza]
hepatitis	hepatit (m)	[hɛpatít]

schizophrenia	skizofreni (f)	[skizofrɛní]
rabies (hydrophobia)	sëmundje e tërbimit (f)	[səmúndjɛ ɛ tərbímit]
neurosis	neurozë (f)	[nɛurózə]
concussion	tronditje (f)	[trondítjɛ]

| cancer | kancer (m) | [kantsér] |
| sclerosis | sklerozë (f) | [sklɛrózə] |

multiple sclerosis	**sklerozë e shumëfishtë** (f)	[sklɛrózə ɛ ʃuməfíʃtə]
alcoholism	**alkoolizëm** (m)	[alkoolízəm]
alcoholic (n)	**alkoolik** (m)	[alkoolík]
syphilis	**sifiliz** (m)	[sifilíz]
AIDS	**SIDA** (f)	[sída]

tumour	**tumor** (m)	[tumóɾ]
malignant (adj)	**malinj**	[malíɲ]
benign (adj)	**beninj**	[bɛníɲ]

fever	**ethe** (f)	[éθɛ]
malaria	**malarie** (f)	[malaríɛ]
gangrene	**gangrenë** (f)	[gaɲrénə]
seasickness	**sëmundje deti** (f)	[səmúndjɛ déti]
epilepsy	**epilepsi** (f)	[ɛpilɛpsí]

epidemic	**epidemi** (f)	[ɛpidɛmí]
typhus	**tifo** (f)	[tífo]
tuberculosis	**tuberkuloz** (f)	[tubɛrkulóz]
cholera	**kolerë** (f)	[kolérə]
plague (bubonic ~)	**murtaja** (f)	[murtája]

64. Symptoms. Treatments. Part 1

symptom	**simptomë** (f)	[simptómə]
temperature	**temperaturë** (f)	[tɛmpɛratúrə]
high temperature (fever)	**temperaturë e lartë** (f)	[tɛmpɛratúrə ɛ lártə]
pulse (heartbeat)	**puls** (m)	[puls]

dizziness (vertigo)	**marrje mendsh** (m)	[márjɛ méndʃ]
hot (adj)	**i nxehtë**	[i ndzéhtə]
shivering	**drithërima** (f)	[driθəríma]
pale (e.g. ~ face)	**i zbehur**	[i zbéhuɾ]

cough	**kollë** (f)	[kóɬə]
to cough (vi)	**kollitem**	[koɬítɛm]
to sneeze (vi)	**teshtij**	[tɛʃtíj]
faint	**të fikët** (f)	[tə fíkət]
to faint (vi)	**bie të fikët**	[bíɛ tə fíkət]

bruise (hématome)	**mavijosje** (f)	[mavijósjɛ]
bump (lump)	**gungë** (f)	[gúɲə]
to bang (bump)	**godas**	[godás]
contusion (bruise)	**lëndim** (m)	[ləndím]
to get a bruise	**lëndohem**	[ləndóhɛm]

to limp (vi)	**çaloj**	[tʃalój]
dislocation	**dislokim** (m)	[dislokím]
to dislocate (vt)	**del nga vendi**	[dɛl ŋa véndi]
fracture	**thyerje** (f)	[θýɛrjɛ]
to have a fracture	**thyej**	[θýɛj]

cut (e.g. paper ~)	**e prerë** (f)	[ɛ prérə]
to cut oneself	**pres veten**	[prɛs vétɛn]

bleeding	rrjedhje gjaku (f)	[rjéðjɛ ɟáku]
burn (injury)	djegie (f)	[djégiɛ]
to get burned	digjem	[díɟɛm]

to prick (vt)	shpoj	[ʃpoj]
to prick oneself	shpohem	[ʃpóhɛm]
to injure (vt)	dëmtoj	[dəmtój]
injury	dëmtim (m)	[dəmtím]
wound	plagë (f)	[plágə]
trauma	traumë (f)	[traúmə]

to be delirious	fol përçart	[fól pərtʃárt]
to stutter (vi)	belbëzoj	[bɛlbəzój]
sunstroke	pikë e diellit (f)	[píkə ɛ diéɫit]

65. Symptoms. Treatments. Part 2

| pain, ache | dhimbje (f) | [ðímbjɛ] |
| splinter (in foot, etc.) | cifël (f) | [tsífəl] |

sweat (perspiration)	djersë (f)	[djérsə]
to sweat (perspire)	djersij	[djɛrsíj]
vomiting	të vjella (f)	[tə vjéɫa]
convulsions	konvulsione (f)	[konvulsiónɛ]

pregnant (adj)	shtatzënë	[ʃtatzə́nə]
to be born	lind	[lind]
delivery, labour	lindje (f)	[líndjɛ]
to deliver (~ a baby)	sjell në jetë	[sjɛɫ nə jétə]
abortion	abort (m)	[abórt]

breathing, respiration	frymëmarrje (f)	[fryməmárjɛ]
in-breath (inhalation)	mbajtje e frymës (f)	[mbájtjɛ ɛ frýməs]
out-breath (exhalation)	lëshim i frymës (m)	[ləʃím i frýməs]
to exhale (breathe out)	nxjerr frymën	[ndzjér frýmən]
to inhale (vi)	marr frymë	[mar frýmə]

disabled person	invalid (m)	[invalíd]
cripple	i gjymtuar (m)	[i ɟymtúar]
drug addict	narkoman (m)	[narkomán]

deaf (adj)	shurdh	[ʃurð]
mute (adj)	memec	[mɛméts]
deaf mute (adj)	shurdh-memec	[ʃurð-mɛméts]

mad, insane (adj)	i marrë	[i márə]
madman (demented person)	i çmendur (m)	[i tʃméndur]
madwoman	e çmendur (f)	[ɛ tʃméndur]
to go insane	çmendem	[tʃméndɛm]

gene	gen (m)	[gɛn]
immunity	imunitet (m)	[imunitét]
hereditary (adj)	e trashëguar	[ɛ traʃəgúar]

congenital (adj)	e lindur	[ɛ líndur]
virus	virus (m)	[virús]
microbe	mikrob (m)	[mikrób]
bacterium	bakterie (f)	[baktériɛ]
infection	infeksion (m)	[infɛksión]

66. Symptoms. Treatments. Part 3

| hospital | spital (m) | [spitál] |
| patient | pacient (m) | [patsiént] |

diagnosis	diagnozë (f)	[diagnózə]
cure	kurë (f)	[kúrə]
medical treatment	trajtim mjekësor (m)	[trajtím mjɛkəsór]
to get treatment	kurohem	[kuróhɛm]
to treat (~ a patient)	kuroj	[kurój]
to nurse (look after)	kujdesem	[kujdésɛm]
care (nursing ~)	kujdes (m)	[kujdés]

operation, surgery	operacion (m)	[opɛratsión]
to bandage (head, limb)	fashoj	[faʃój]
bandaging	fashim (m)	[faʃím]

vaccination	vaksinim (m)	[vaksiním]
to vaccinate (vt)	vaksinoj	[vaksinój]
injection	injeksion (m)	[iɲɛksión]
to give an injection	bëj injeksion	[bəj iɲɛksíon]

attack	atak (m)	[aták]
amputation	amputim (m)	[amputím]
to amputate (vt)	amputoj	[amputój]
coma	komë (f)	[kómə]
to be in a coma	jam në komë	[jam nə kómə]
intensive care	kujdes intensiv (m)	[kujdés intɛnsív]

to recover (~ from flu)	shërohem	[ʃəróhɛm]
condition (patient's ~)	gjendje (f)	[ɟéndjɛ]
consciousness	vetëdije (f)	[vɛtədíjɛ]
memory (faculty)	kujtesë (f)	[kujtésə]

to pull out (tooth)	heq	[hɛc]
filling	mbushje (f)	[mbúʃɛ]
to fill (a tooth)	mbush	[mbúʃ]

| hypnosis | hipnozë (f) | [hipnózə] |
| to hypnotize (vt) | hipnotizim | [hipnotizím] |

67. Medicine. Drugs. Accessories

medicine, drug	ilaç (m)	[ilátʃ]
remedy	mjekim (m)	[mjɛkím]
to prescribe (vt)	shkruaj recetë	[ʃkrúaj rɛtsétə]

prescription	recetë (f)	[rɛtsétə]
tablet, pill	pilulë (f)	[pilúlə]
ointment	krem (m)	[krɛm]
ampoule	ampulë (f)	[ampúlə]
mixture, solution	përzierje (f)	[pərzíɛrjɛ]
syrup	shurup (m)	[ʃurúp]
capsule	pilulë (f)	[pilúlə]
powder	pudër (f)	[púdər]

gauze bandage	fashë garze (f)	[faʃə gárzɛ]
cotton wool	pambuk (m)	[pambúk]
iodine	jod (m)	[jod]

plaster	leukoplast (m)	[lɛukoplást]
eyedropper	pikatore (f)	[pikatórɛ]
thermometer	termometër (m)	[tɛrmométər]
syringe	shiringë (f)	[ʃiríŋə]

| wheelchair | karrocë me rrota (f) | [karótsə mɛ róta] |
| crutches | paterica (f) | [patɛrítsa] |

painkiller	qetësues (m)	[cɛtəsúɛs]
laxative	laksativ (m)	[laksatív]
spirits (ethanol)	alkool dezinfektues (m)	[alkoól dɛzinfɛktúɛs]
medicinal herbs	bimë mjekësore (f)	[bímə mjɛkəsórɛ]
herbal (~ tea)	çaj bimor	[tʃáj bimór]

FLAT

68. Flat

flat	apartament (m)	[apartamént]
room	dhomë (f)	[ðómə]
bedroom	dhomë gjumi (f)	[ðómə ɟúmi]
dining room	dhomë ngrënie (f)	[ðómə ŋrəníɛ]
living room	dhomë ndeje (f)	[ðómə ndéjɛ]
study (home office)	dhomë pune (f)	[ðómə púnɛ]
entry room	hyrje (f)	[hýrjɛ]
bathroom	banjo (f)	[báɲo]
water closet	tualet (m)	[tualét]
ceiling	tavan (m)	[taván]
floor	dysheme (f)	[dyʃɛmé]
corner	qoshe (f)	[cóʃɛ]

69. Furniture. Interior

furniture	orendi (f)	[orɛndí]
table	tryezë (f)	[tryézə]
chair	karrige (f)	[karígɛ]
bed	shtrat (m)	[ʃtrat]
sofa, settee	divan (m)	[diván]
armchair	kolltuk (m)	[koɬtúk]
bookcase	raft librash (m)	[ráft líbraʃ]
shelf	sergjen (m)	[sɛrɟén]
wardrobe	garderobë (f)	[gardəróbə]
coat rack (wall-mounted ~)	varëse (f)	[várəsɛ]
coat stand	varëse xhaketash (f)	[várəsɛ dʒakétaʃ]
chest of drawers	komodë (f)	[komódə]
coffee table	tryezë e ulët (f)	[tryézə ɛ úlət]
mirror	pasqyrë (f)	[pascýrə]
carpet	qilim (m)	[cilím]
small carpet	tapet (m)	[tapét]
fireplace	oxhak (m)	[odʒák]
candle	qiri (m)	[círi]
candlestick	shandan (m)	[ʃandán]
drapes	perde (f)	[pérdɛ]
wallpaper	tapiceri (f)	[tapitsɛrí]

blinds (jalousie)	grila (f)	[gríla]
table lamp	llambë tavoline (f)	[ɫámbə tavolínɛ]
wall lamp (sconce)	llambadar muri (m)	[ɫambadár múri]
standard lamp	llambadar (m)	[ɫambadár]
chandelier	llambadar (m)	[ɫambadár]
leg (of a chair, table)	këmbë (f)	[kə́mbə]
armrest	mbështetëse krahu (f)	[mbəʃtétəsɛ kráhu]
back (backrest)	mbështetëse (f)	[mbəʃtétəsɛ]
drawer	sirtar (m)	[sirtár]

70. Bedding

bedclothes	çarçafë (pl)	[tʃartʃáfə]
pillow	jastëk (m)	[jastə́k]
pillowslip	këllëf jastëku (m)	[kəɫə́f jastə́ku]
duvet	jorgan (m)	[jorgán]
sheet	çarçaf (m)	[tʃartʃáf]
bedspread	mbulesë (f)	[mbulésə]

71. Kitchen

kitchen	kuzhinë (f)	[kuʒínə]
gas	gaz (m)	[gaz]
gas cooker	sobë me gaz (f)	[sóbə mɛ gaz]
electric cooker	sobë elektrike (f)	[sóbə ɛlɛktríkɛ]
oven	furrë (f)	[fúrə]
microwave oven	mikrovalë (f)	[mikroválə]
refrigerator	frigorifer (m)	[frigorifér]
freezer	frigorifer (m)	[frigorifér]
dishwasher	pjatalarëse (f)	[pjatalárəsɛ]
mincer	grirëse mishi (f)	[grírəsɛ míʃi]
juicer	shtrydhëse frutash (f)	[ʃtrýðəsɛ frútaʃ]
toaster	toster (m)	[tostér]
mixer	mikser (m)	[miksér]
coffee machine	makinë kafeje (f)	[makínə kaféjɛ]
coffee pot	kafetierë (f)	[kafɛtiérə]
coffee grinder	mulli kafeje (f)	[muɫí káfɛjɛ]
kettle	çajnik (m)	[tʃajník]
teapot	çajnik (m)	[tʃajník]
lid	kapak (m)	[kapák]
tea strainer	sitë çaji (f)	[sítə tʃáji]
spoon	lugë (f)	[lúgə]
teaspoon	lugë çaji (f)	[lúgə tʃáji]
soup spoon	lugë gjelle (f)	[lúgə ɟéɫɛ]
fork	pirun (m)	[pirún]
knife	thikë (f)	[θíkə]

tableware (dishes)	enë kuzhine (f)	[énǝ kuʒínɛ]
plate (dinner ~)	pjatë (f)	[pjátǝ]
saucer	pjatë filxhani (f)	[pjátǝ fildʒáni]

shot glass	potir (m)	[potír]
glass (tumbler)	gotë (f)	[gótǝ]
cup	filxhan (m)	[fildʒán]

sugar bowl	tas për sheqer (m)	[tas pǝr ʃɛcér]
salt cellar	kripore (f)	[kripórɛ]
pepper pot	enë piperi (f)	[énǝ pipéri]
butter dish	pjatë gjalpi (f)	[pjátǝ ɟálpi]

stock pot (soup pot)	tenxhere (f)	[tɛndʒérɛ]
frying pan (skillet)	tigan (m)	[tigán]
ladle	garuzhdë (f)	[garúʒdǝ]
colander	kullesë (f)	[kuɫésǝ]
tray (serving ~)	tabaka (f)	[tabaká]

bottle	shishe (f)	[ʃíʃɛ]
jar (glass)	kavanoz (m)	[kavanóz]
tin (can)	kanoçe (f)	[kanótʃɛ]

bottle opener	hapëse shishesh (f)	[hapǝsé ʃíʃɛʃ]
tin opener	hapëse kanoçesh (f)	[hapǝsé kanótʃɛʃ]
corkscrew	turjelë tapash (f)	[turjélǝ tápaʃ]
filter	filtër (m)	[fíltǝr]
to filter (vt)	filtroj	[filtrój]

waste (food ~, etc.)	pleh (m)	[plɛh]
waste bin (kitchen ~)	kosh plehrash (m)	[koʃ pléhraʃ]

72. Bathroom

bathroom	banjo (f)	[báɲo]
water	ujë (m)	[újǝ]
tap	rubinet (m)	[rubinét]
hot water	ujë i nxehtë (f)	[újǝ i ndzéhtǝ]
cold water	ujë i ftohtë (f)	[újǝ i ftóhtǝ]

toothpaste	pastë dhëmbësh (f)	[pástǝ ðémbǝʃ]
to clean one's teeth	laj dhëmbët	[laj ðémbǝt]
toothbrush	furçë dhëmbësh (f)	[fúrtʃǝ ðémbǝʃ]

to shave (vi)	rruhem	[rúhɛm]
shaving foam	shkumë rroje (f)	[ʃkumǝ rójɛ]
razor	brisk (m)	[brísk]

to wash (one's hands, etc.)	laj duart	[laj dúart]
to have a bath	lahem	[láhɛm]
shower	dush (m)	[duʃ]
to have a shower	bëj dush	[bǝj dúʃ]
bath	vaskë (f)	[váskǝ]
toilet (toilet bowl)	tualet (m)	[tualét]

sink (washbasin)	**lavaman** (m)	[lavamán]
soap	**sapun** (m)	[sapún]
soap dish	**pjatë sapuni** (f)	[pjátə sapúni]
sponge	**sfungjer** (m)	[sfunɟér]
shampoo	**shampo** (f)	[ʃampó]
towel	**peshqir** (m)	[pɛʃcír]
bathrobe	**peshqir trupi** (m)	[pɛʃcír trúpi]
laundry (laundering)	**larje** (f)	[lárjɛ]
washing machine	**makinë larëse** (f)	[makínə lárəsɛ]
to do the laundry	**laj rroba**	[laj róba]
washing powder	**detergjent** (m)	[dɛtɛɲént]

73. Household appliances

TV, telly	**televizor** (m)	[tɛlɛvizór]
tape recorder	**inçizues me shirit** (m)	[intʃizúɛs mɛ ʃirít]
video	**video regjistrues** (m)	[vídɛo rɛɟistrúɛs]
radio	**radio** (f)	[rádio]
player (CD, MP3, etc.)	**kasetofon** (m)	[kasɛtofón]
video projector	**projektor** (m)	[projɛktór]
home cinema	**kinema shtëpie** (f)	[kinɛmá ʃtəpíɛ]
DVD player	**DVD player** (m)	[dividí plɛjər]
amplifier	**amplifikator** (m)	[amplifikatór]
video game console	**konsol video loje** (m)	[konsól vídɛo lójɛ]
video camera	**videokamerë** (f)	[vidɛokamérə]
camera (photo)	**aparat fotografik** (m)	[aparát fotografík]
digital camera	**kamerë digjitale** (f)	[kamérə diɟitálɛ]
vacuum cleaner	**fshesë elektrike** (f)	[fʃésə ɛlɛktríkɛ]
iron (e.g. steam ~)	**hekur** (m)	[hékur]
ironing board	**tryezë për hekurosje** (f)	[tryézə pər hɛkurósjɛ]
telephone	**telefon** (m)	[tɛlɛfón]
mobile phone	**celular** (m)	[tsɛlulár]
typewriter	**makinë shkrimi** (f)	[makínə ʃkrími]
sewing machine	**makinë qepëse** (f)	[makínə cépəsɛ]
microphone	**mikrofon** (m)	[mikrofón]
headphones	**kufje** (f)	[kúfjɛ]
remote control (TV)	**telekomandë** (f)	[tɛlɛkomándə]
CD, compact disc	**CD** (f)	[tsɛdé]
cassette, tape	**kasetë** (f)	[kasétə]
vinyl record	**pllakë gramafoni** (f)	[pɫákə gramafóni]

THE EARTH. WEATHER

74. Outer space

space	hapësirë (f)	[hapəsírə]
space (as adj)	hapësinor	[hapəsinór]
outer space	kozmos (m)	[kozmós]

world	botë (f)	[bótə]
universe	univers	[univérs]
galaxy	galaksi (f)	[galaksí]

star	yll (m)	[yɫ]
constellation	yllësi (f)	[yɫəsí]
planet	planet (m)	[planét]
satellite	satelit (m)	[satɛlít]

meteorite	meteor (m)	[mɛtɛór]
comet	kometë (f)	[kométə]
asteroid	asteroid (m)	[astɛroíd]

orbit	orbitë (f)	[orbítə]
to revolve (~ around the Earth)	rrotullohet	[rrotuɫóhɛt]
atmosphere	atmosferë (f)	[atmosférə]

the Sun	Dielli (m)	[diéɫi]
solar system	sistemi diellor (m)	[sistémi diɛɫór]
solar eclipse	eklips diellor (m)	[ɛklíps diɛɫór]

| the Earth | Toka (f) | [tóka] |
| the Moon | Hëna (f) | [héna] |

Mars	Marsi (m)	[mársi]
Venus	Venera (f)	[vɛnéra]
Jupiter	Jupiteri (m)	[jupitéri]
Saturn	Saturni (m)	[satúrni]

Mercury	Merkuri (m)	[mɛrkúri]
Uranus	Urani (m)	[uráni]
Neptune	Neptuni (m)	[nɛptúni]
Pluto	Pluto (f)	[plúto]

Milky Way	Rruga e Qumështit (f)	[rúga ɛ cúməʃtit]
Great Bear (Ursa Major)	Arusha e Madhe (f)	[arúʃa ɛ máðɛ]
North Star	ylli i Veriut (m)	[ýɫi i vériut]

Martian	Marsian (m)	[marsián]
extraterrestrial (n)	jashtëtokësor (m)	[jaʃtetokəsór]
alien	alien (m)	[alién]

flying saucer	disk fluturues (m)	[dísk fluturúɛs]
spaceship	anije kozmike (f)	[aníjɛ kozmíkɛ]
space station	stacion kozmik (m)	[statsión kozmík]
blast-off	ngritje (f)	[ŋrítjɛ]

engine	motor (m)	[motór]
nozzle	dizë (f)	[dízə]
fuel	karburant (m)	[karburánt]

| cockpit, flight deck | kabinë pilotimi (f) | [kabínə pilotími] |
| aerial | antenë (f) | [anténə] |

porthole	dritare anësore (f)	[dritárɛ anəsórɛ]
solar panel	panel solar (m)	[panél solár]
spacesuit	veshje astronauti (f)	[véʃjɛ astronáuti]

| weightlessness | mungesë graviteti (f) | [muŋésə gravitéti] |
| oxygen | oksigjen (m) | [oksiɟén] |

| docking (in space) | ndërlidhje në hapësirë (f) | [ndərlíðjɛ nə hapəsírə] |
| to dock (vi, vt) | stacionohem | [statsionóhɛm] |

| observatory | observator (m) | [obsɛrvatór] |
| telescope | teleskop (m) | [tɛlɛskóp] |

| to observe (vt) | vëzhgoj | [vəʒgój] |
| to explore (vt) | eksploroj | [ɛksplorój] |

75. The Earth

the Earth	Toka (f)	[tóka]
the globe (the Earth)	globi (f)	[glóbi]
planet	planet (m)	[planét]

atmosphere	atmosferë (f)	[atmosférə]
geography	gjeografi (f)	[ɟɛografí]
nature	natyrë (f)	[natýrə]

globe (table ~)	glob (m)	[glob]
map	hartë (f)	[hártə]
atlas	atlas (m)	[atlás]

| Europe | Evropa (f) | [ɛvrópa] |
| Asia | Azia (f) | [azía] |

| Africa | Afrika (f) | [afríka] |
| Australia | Australia (f) | [australía] |

America	Amerika (f)	[amɛríka]
North America	Amerika Veriore (f)	[amɛríka vɛriórɛ]
South America	Amerika Jugore (f)	[amɛríka jugórɛ]

| Antarctica | Antarktika (f) | [antarktíka] |
| the Arctic | Arktiku (m) | [arktíku] |

76. Cardinal directions

north	veri (m)	[vɛrí]
to the north	drejt veriut	[dréjt vériut]
in the north	në veri	[nə vɛrí]
northern (adj)	verior	[vɛriór]

south	jug (m)	[jug]
to the south	drejt jugut	[dréjt júgut]
in the south	në jug	[nə jug]
southern (adj)	jugor	[jugór]

west	perëndim (m)	[pɛrəndím]
to the west	drejt perëndimit	[dréjt pɛrəndímit]
in the west	në perëndim	[nə pɛrəndím]
western (adj)	perëndimor	[pɛrəndimór]

east	lindje (f)	[líndjɛ]
to the east	drejt lindjes	[dréjt líndjɛs]
in the east	në lindje	[nə líndjɛ]
eastern (adj)	lindor	[lindór]

77. Sea. Ocean

sea	det (m)	[dét]
ocean	oqean (m)	[ocɛán]
gulf (bay)	gji (m)	[ɟi]
straits	ngushticë (f)	[ŋuʃtítsə]

land (solid ground)	tokë (f)	[tókə]
continent (mainland)	kontinent (m)	[kontinént]

island	ishull (m)	[íʃuɬ]
peninsula	gadishull (m)	[gadíʃuɬ]
archipelago	arkipelag (m)	[arkipɛlág]

bay, cove	gji (m)	[ɟi]
harbour	port (m)	[port]
lagoon	lagunë (f)	[lagúnə]
cape	kep (m)	[kɛp]

atoll	atol (m)	[atól]
reef	shkëmb nënujor (m)	[ʃkəmb nənujór]
coral	koral (m)	[korál]
coral reef	korale nënujorë (f)	[korálɛ nənujórə]

deep (adj)	i thellë	[i θéɬə]
depth (deep water)	thellësi (f)	[θɛɬəsí]
abyss	humnerë (f)	[humnérə]
trench (e.g. Mariana ~)	hendek (m)	[hɛndék]

current (Ocean ~)	rrymë (f)	[rýmə]
to surround (bathe)	rrethohet	[rɛθóhɛt]

| shore | breg (m) | [brɛg] |
| coast | bregdet (m) | [brɛgdét] |

flow (flood tide)	batica (f)	[batítsa]
ebb (ebb tide)	zbaticë (f)	[zbatítsə]
shoal	cekëtinë (f)	[tsɛkətínə]
bottom (~ of the sea)	fund i detit (m)	[fúnd i détit]

wave	dallgë (f)	[dáɫgə]
crest (~ of a wave)	kreshtë (f)	[kréʃtə]
spume (sea foam)	shkumë (f)	[ʃkúmə]

storm (sea storm)	stuhi (f)	[stuhí]
hurricane	uragan (m)	[uragán]
tsunami	cunam (m)	[tsunám]
calm (dead ~)	qetësi (f)	[cɛtəsí]
quiet, calm (adj)	i qetë	[i cétə]

| pole | pol (m) | [pol] |
| polar (adj) | polar | [polár] |

latitude	gjerësi (f)	[ɟɛrəsí]
longitude	gjatësi (f)	[ɟatəsí]
parallel	paralele (f)	[paralélɛ]
equator	ekuator (m)	[ɛkuatór]

sky	qiell (m)	[cíɛɫ]
horizon	horizont (m)	[horizónt]
air	ajër (m)	[ájər]

lighthouse	fanar (m)	[fanár]
to dive (vi)	zhytem	[ʒýtɛm]
to sink (ab. boat)	fundosje	[fundósjɛ]
treasure	thesare (pl)	[θɛsárɛ]

78. Seas & Oceans names

Atlantic Ocean	Oqeani Atlantik (m)	[ocɛáni atlantík]
Indian Ocean	Oqeani Indian (m)	[ocɛáni indián]
Pacific Ocean	Oqeani Paqësor (m)	[ocɛáni pacəsór]
Arctic Ocean	Oqeani Arktik (m)	[ocɛáni arktík]

Black Sea	Deti i Zi (m)	[déti i zí]
Red Sea	Deti i Kuq (m)	[déti i kúc]
Yellow Sea	Deti i Verdhë (m)	[déti i vérðə]
White Sea	Deti i Bardhë (m)	[déti i bárðə]

Caspian Sea	Deti Kaspik (m)	[déti kaspík]
Dead Sea	Deti i Vdekur (m)	[déti i vdékur]
Mediterranean Sea	Deti Mesdhe (m)	[déti mɛsðé]

Aegean Sea	Deti Egje (m)	[déti ɛɟé]
Adriatic Sea	Deti Adriatik (m)	[déti adriatík]
Arabian Sea	Deti Arab (m)	[déti aráb]

Sea of Japan	Deti i Japonisë (m)	[déti i japonísə]
Bering Sea	Deti Bering (m)	[déti bériŋ]
South China Sea	Deti i Kinës Jugore (m)	[déti i kínəs jugórɛ]

Coral Sea	Deti Koral (m)	[déti korál]
Tasman Sea	Deti Tasman (m)	[déti tasmán]
Caribbean Sea	Deti i Karaibeve (m)	[déti i karaíbɛvɛ]

| Barents Sea | Deti Barents (m) | [déti barénts] |
| Kara Sea | Deti Kara (m) | [déti kára] |

North Sea	Deti i Veriut (m)	[déti i vériut]
Baltic Sea	Deti Baltik (m)	[déti baltík]
Norwegian Sea	Deti Norvegjez (m)	[déti norvɛɟéz]

79. Mountains

mountain	mal (m)	[mal]
mountain range	vargmal (m)	[vargmál]
mountain ridge	kresht malor (m)	[kréʃt malór]

summit, top	majë (f)	[májə]
peak	maja më e lartë (f)	[mája mə ɛ lártə]
foot (~ of the mountain)	rrëza e malit (f)	[rəza ɛ málit]
slope (mountainside)	shpat (m)	[ʃpat]

volcano	vullkan (m)	[vuɫkán]
active volcano	vullkan aktiv (m)	[vuɫkán aktív]
dormant volcano	vullkan i fjetur (m)	[vuɫkán i fjétur]

eruption	shpërthim (m)	[ʃpərθím]
crater	krater (m)	[kratér]
magma	magmë (f)	[mágmə]
lava	llavë (f)	[ɫávə]
molten (~ lava)	i shkrirë	[i ʃkrírə]

canyon	kanion (m)	[kanión]
gorge	grykë (f)	[grýkə]
crevice	çarje (f)	[tʃárjɛ]
abyss (chasm)	humnerë (f)	[humnérə]

pass, col	kalim (m)	[kalím]
plateau	pllajë (f)	[pɫájə]
cliff	shkëmb (m)	[ʃkəmb]
hill	kodër (f)	[kódər]

glacier	akullnajë (f)	[akuɫnájə]
waterfall	ujëvarë (f)	[ujəvárə]
geyser	gejzer (m)	[gɛjzér]
lake	liqen (m)	[licén]

plain	fushë (f)	[fúʃə]
landscape	peizazh (m)	[pɛizáʒ]
echo	jehonë (f)	[jɛhónə]

alpinist	alpinist (m)	[alpiníst]
rock climber	alpinist shkëmbßinjsh (m)	[alpiníst ʃkəmbiɲʃ]
to conquer (in climbing)	pushtoj majën	[puʃtój májən]
climb (an easy ~)	ngjitje (f)	[ɲɟítjɛ]

80. Mountains names

The Alps	Alpet (pl)	[alpét]
Mont Blanc	Montblanc (m)	[montblánk]
The Pyrenees	Pirenejet (pl)	[pirɛnéjɛt]

The Carpathians	Karpatet (m)	[karpátɛt]
The Ural Mountains	Malet Urale (pl)	[málɛt urálɛ]
The Caucasus Mountains	Malet Kaukaze (pl)	[málɛt kaukázɛ]
Mount Elbrus	Mali Elbrus (m)	[máli ɛlbrús]

The Altai Mountains	Malet Altai (pl)	[málɛt altái]
The Tian Shan	Tian Shani (m)	[tían ʃáni]
The Pamirs	Malet e Pamirit (m)	[málɛt ɛ pamírit]
The Himalayas	Himalajet (pl)	[himalájɛt]
Mount Everest	Mali Everest (m)	[máli ɛvɛrést]

| The Andes | andet (pl) | [ándɛt] |
| Mount Kilimanjaro | Mali Kilimanxharo (m) | [máli kilimandʒáro] |

81. Rivers

river	lum (m)	[lum]
spring (natural source)	burim (m)	[burím]
riverbed (river channel)	shtrat lumi (m)	[ʃtrat lúmi]
basin (river valley)	basen (m)	[basén]
to flow into ...	rrjedh ...	[rjéð ...]

| tributary | derdhje (f) | [dérðjɛ] |
| bank (river ~) | breg (m) | [brɛg] |

current (stream)	rrymë (f)	[rýmə]
downstream (adv)	rrjedhje e poshtme	[rjéðjɛ ɛ póʃtmɛ]
upstream (adv)	rrjedhje e sipërme	[rjéðjɛ ɛ sípərmɛ]

inundation	vërshim (m)	[vərʃím]
flooding	përmbytje (f)	[pərmbýtjɛ]
to overflow (vi)	vërshon	[vərʃón]
to flood (vt)	përmbytet	[pərmbýtɛt]

| shallow (shoal) | cekëtinë (f) | [tsɛkətínə] |
| rapids | rrjedhë (f) | [rjéðə] |

dam	digë (f)	[dígə]
canal	kanal (m)	[kanál]
reservoir (artificial lake)	rezervuar (m)	[rɛzɛrvuár]
sluice, lock	pendë ujore (f)	[péndə ujórɛ]

water body (pond, etc.)	plan hidrik (m)	[plan hidrík]
swamp (marshland)	kënetë (f)	[kənétə]
bog, marsh	moçal (m)	[motʃ ál]
whirlpool	vorbull (f)	[vórbuɫ]

stream (brook)	përrua (f)	[pərúa]
drinking (ab. water)	i pijshëm	[i píjʃəm]
fresh (~ water)	i freskët	[i fréskət]

| ice | akull (m) | [ákuɫ] |
| to freeze over (ab. river, etc.) | ngrihet | [ŋríhɛt] |

82. Rivers names

| Seine | Sena (f) | [séna] |
| Loire | Loire (f) | [luar] |

Thames	Temza (f)	[témza]
Rhine	Rajnë (m)	[rájnə]
Danube	Danubi (m)	[danúbi]

Volga	Volga (f)	[vólga]
Don	Doni (m)	[dóni]
Lena	Lena (f)	[léna]

Yellow River	Lumi i Verdhë (m)	[lúmi i vérðə]
Yangtze	Jangce (f)	[jaŋtsé]
Mekong	Mekong (m)	[mɛkóŋ]
Ganges	Gang (m)	[gaŋ]

Nile River	Lumi Nil (m)	[lúmi nil]
Congo River	Lumi Kongo (m)	[lúmi kóŋo]
Okavango River	Lumi Okavango (m)	[lúmi okaváŋo]
Zambezi River	Lumi Zambezi (m)	[lúmi zambézi]
Limpopo River	Lumi Limpopo (m)	[lúmi limpópo]
Mississippi River	Lumi Misisipi (m)	[lúmi misisípi]

83. Forest

| forest, wood | pyll (m) | [pyɫ] |
| forest (as adj) | pyjor | [pyjór] |

thick forest	pyll i ngjeshur (m)	[pyɫ i ɲɟéʃur]
grove	zabel (m)	[zabél]
forest clearing	lëndinë (f)	[ləndínə]

| thicket | pyllëz (m) | [pýɫəz] |
| scrubland | shkurre (f) | [ʃkúrɛ] |

footpath (troddenpath)	shteg (m)	[ʃtɛg]
gully	hon (m)	[hon]
tree	pemë (f)	[pémə]

| leaf | gjeth (m) | [ɟɛθ] |
| leaves (foliage) | gjethe (pl) | [ɟéθɛ] |

fall of leaves	rënie e gjetheve (f)	[rəníɛ ɛ ɟéθɛvɛ]
to fall (ab. leaves)	bien	[bíɛn]
top (of the tree)	maje (f)	[májɛ]

branch	degë (f)	[dégə]
bough	degë (f)	[dégə]
bud (on shrub, tree)	syth (m)	[syθ]
needle (of the pine tree)	shtiza pishe (f)	[ʃtíza píʃɛ]
fir cone	lule pishe (f)	[lúlɛ píʃɛ]

tree hollow	zgavër (f)	[zgávər]
nest	fole (f)	[folé]
burrow (animal hole)	strofull (f)	[strófuɫ]

trunk	trung (m)	[truŋ]
root	rrënjë (f)	[réɲə]
bark	lëvore (f)	[ləvórɛ]
moss	myshk (m)	[myʃk]

to uproot (remove trees or tree stumps)	shkul	[ʃkul]
to chop down	pres	[prɛs]
to deforest (vt)	shpyllëzoj	[ʃpyɫəzój]
tree stump	cung (m)	[tsúŋ]

campfire	zjarr kampingu (m)	[zjar kampíŋu]
forest fire	zjarr në pyll (m)	[zjar nə pyɫ]
to extinguish (vt)	shuaj	[ʃúaj]

forest ranger	roje pyjore (f)	[rójɛ pyjórɛ]
protection	mbrojtje (f)	[mbrójtjɛ]
to protect (~ nature)	mbroj	[mbrój]
poacher	gjahtar i jashtëligjshëm (m)	[ɟahtár i jaʃtəlíɟʃəm]
steel trap	grackë (f)	[grátskə]

| to gather, to pick (vt) | mbledh | [mbléð] |
| to lose one's way | humb rrugën | [húmb rúgən] |

84. Natural resources

natural resources	burime natyrore (pl)	[burímɛ natyrórɛ]
minerals	minerale (pl)	[minɛrálɛ]
deposits	depozita (pl)	[dɛpozíta]
field (e.g. oilfield)	fushë (f)	[fúʃə]

to mine (extract)	nxjerr	[ndzjér]
mining (extraction)	nxjerrje mineralesh (f)	[ndzjérjɛ minɛrálɛʃ]
ore	xehe (f)	[dzéhɛ]
mine (e.g. for coal)	minierë (f)	[miniérə]
shaft (mine ~)	nivel (m)	[nivél]
miner	minator (m)	[minatór]

gas (natural ~)	**gaz** (m)	[gaz]
gas pipeline	**gazsjellës** (m)	[gazsjéɬəs]
oil (petroleum)	**naftë** (f)	[náftə]
oil pipeline	**naftësjellës** (f)	[naftəsjéɬəs]
oil well	**pus nafte** (m)	[pus náftɛ]
derrick (tower)	**burim nafte** (m)	[burím náftɛ]
tanker	**anije-cisternë** (f)	[aníjɛ-tsistérnə]
sand	**rërë** (f)	[rérə]
limestone	**gur gëlqeror** (m)	[gur gəlcɛrór]
gravel	**zhavorr** (m)	[ʒavór]
peat	**torfë** (f)	[tórfə]
clay	**argjilë** (f)	[arɟílə]
coal	**qymyr** (m)	[cymýr]
iron (ore)	**hekur** (m)	[hékur]
gold	**ar** (m)	[ár]
silver	**argjend** (m)	[arɟénd]
nickel	**nikel** (m)	[nikél]
copper	**bakër** (m)	[bákər]
zinc	**zink** (m)	[zink]
manganese	**mangan** (m)	[maŋán]
mercury	**merkur** (m)	[mɛrkúr]
lead	**plumb** (m)	[plúmb]
mineral	**mineral** (m)	[minɛrál]
crystal	**kristal** (m)	[kristál]
marble	**mermer** (m)	[mɛrmér]
uranium	**uranium** (m)	[uraniúm]

85. Weather

weather	**moti** (m)	[móti]
weather forecast	**parashikimi i motit** (m)	[paraʃikími i mótit]
temperature	**temperaturë** (f)	[tɛmpɛratúrə]
thermometer	**termometër** (m)	[tɛrmométər]
barometer	**barometër** (m)	[barométər]
humid (adj)	**i lagësht**	[i lágəʃt]
humidity	**lagështi** (f)	[lagəʃtí]
heat (extreme ~)	**vapë** (f)	[vápə]
hot (torrid)	**shumë nxehtë**	[ʃúmə ndzéhtə]
it's hot	**është nxehtë**	[éʃtə ndzéhtə]
it's warm	**është ngrohtë**	[éʃtə ŋróhtə]
warm (moderately hot)	**ngrohtë**	[ŋróhtə]
it's cold	**bën ftohtë**	[bən ftóhtə]
cold (adj)	**i ftohtë**	[i ftóhtə]
sun	**diell** (m)	[díɛɬ]
to shine (vi)	**ndriçon**	[ndritʃón]

sunny (day)	**me diell**	[mɛ díɛɫ]
to come up (vi)	**agon**	[agón]
to set (vi)	**perëndon**	[pɛrəndón]

cloud	**re** (f)	[rɛ]
cloudy (adj)	**vranët**	[vránət]
rain cloud	**re shiu** (f)	[rɛ ʃíu]
somber (gloomy)	**vranët**	[vránət]

rain	**shi** (m)	[ʃí]
it's raining	**bie shi**	[bíɛ ʃí]
rainy (~ day, weather)	**me shi**	[mɛ ʃí]
to drizzle (vi)	**shi i imët**	[ʃi i ímət]

pouring rain	**shi litar** (m)	[ʃi litár]
downpour	**stuhi shiu** (f)	[stuhí ʃíu]
heavy (e.g. ~ rain)	**i fortë**	[i fórtə]
puddle	**brakë** (f)	[brákə]
to get wet (in rain)	**lagem**	[lágɛm]

fog (mist)	**mjegull** (f)	[mjéguɫ]
foggy	**e mjegullt**	[ɛ mjéguɫt]
snow	**borë** (f)	[bórə]
it's snowing	**bie borë**	[bíɛ bórə]

86. Severe weather. Natural disasters

thunderstorm	**stuhi** (f)	[stuhí]
lightning (~ strike)	**vetëtimë** (f)	[vɛtətímə]
to flash (vi)	**vetëton**	[vɛtətón]

thunder	**bubullimë** (f)	[bubuɫímə]
to thunder (vi)	**bubullon**	[bubuɫón]
it's thundering	**bubullon**	[bubuɫón]

hail	**breshër** (m)	[bréʃər]
it's hailing	**po bie breshër**	[po biɛ bréʃər]

to flood (vt)	**përmbytet**	[pərmbýtɛt]
flood, inundation	**përmbytje** (f)	[pərmbýtjɛ]

earthquake	**tërmet** (m)	[tərmét]
tremor, shoke	**lëkundje** (f)	[ləkúndjɛ]
epicentre	**epiqendër** (f)	[ɛpicéndər]

eruption	**shpërthim** (m)	[ʃpərθím]
lava	**llavë** (f)	[ɫávə]

twister	**vorbull** (f)	[vórbuɫ]
tornado	**tornado** (f)	[tornádo]
typhoon	**tajfun** (m)	[tajfún]

hurricane	**uragan** (m)	[uragán]
storm	**stuhi** (f)	[stuhí]

tsunami	**cunam** (m)	[tsunám]
cyclone	**ciklon** (m)	[tsiklón]
bad weather	**mot i keq** (m)	[mot i kɛc]
fire (accident)	**zjarr** (m)	[zjar]
disaster	**fatkeqësi** (f)	[fatkɛcəsí]
meteorite	**meteor** (m)	[mɛtɛór]
avalanche	**ortek** (m)	[orték]
snowslide	**rrëshqitje bore** (f)	[rəʃcítjɛ bórɛ]
blizzard	**stuhi bore** (f)	[stuhí bórɛ]
snowstorm	**stuhi bore** (f)	[stuhí bórɛ]

FAUNA

87. Mammals. Predators

predator	**grabitqar** (m)	[grabitcár]
tiger	**tigër** (m)	[tígər]
lion	**luan** (m)	[luán]
wolf	**ujk** (m)	[ujk]
fox	**dhelpër** (f)	[ðélpər]
jaguar	**jaguar** (m)	[jaguár]
leopard	**leopard** (m)	[lɛopárd]
cheetah	**gepard** (m)	[gɛpárd]
black panther	**panterë e zezë** (f)	[pantérə ɛ zézə]
puma	**puma** (f)	[púma]
snow leopard	**leopard i borës** (m)	[lɛopárd i bórəs]
lynx	**rrëqebull** (m)	[rəcébuɫ]
coyote	**kojotë** (f)	[kojótə]
jackal	**çakall** (m)	[tʃakáɫ]
hyena	**hienë** (f)	[hiénə]

88. Wild animals

animal	**kafshë** (f)	[káfʃə]
beast (animal)	**bishë** (f)	[bíʃə]
squirrel	**ketër** (m)	[kétər]
hedgehog	**iriq** (m)	[iríc]
hare	**lepur i egër** (m)	[lépur i égər]
rabbit	**lepur** (m)	[lépur]
badger	**vjedull** (f)	[vjéduɫ]
raccoon	**rakun** (m)	[rakún]
hamster	**hamster** (m)	[hamstér]
marmot	**marmot** (m)	[marmót]
mole	**urith** (m)	[uríθ]
mouse	**mi** (m)	[mi]
rat	**mi** (m)	[mi]
bat	**lakuriq** (m)	[lakuríc]
ermine	**herminë** (f)	[hɛrmínə]
sable	**kunadhe** (f)	[kunáðɛ]
marten	**shqarth** (m)	[ʃcarθ]
weasel	**nuselalë** (f)	[nusɛlálə]
mink	**vizon** (m)	[vizón]

| beaver | kastor (m) | [kastór] |
| otter | vidër (f) | [vídər] |

horse	kali (m)	[káli]
moose	dre brilopatë (m)	[drɛ brilopátə]
deer	dre (f)	[drɛ]
camel	deve (f)	[dévɛ]

bison	bizon (m)	[bizón]
wisent	bizon evropian (m)	[bizón ɛvropián]
buffalo	buall (m)	[búatɬ]

zebra	zebër (f)	[zébər]
antelope	antilopë (f)	[antilópə]
roe deer	dre (f)	[drɛ]
fallow deer	dre ugar (m)	[drɛ ugár]
chamois	kamosh (m)	[kamóʃ]
wild boar	derr i egër (m)	[dér i égər]

whale	balenë (f)	[balénə]
seal	fokë (f)	[fókə]
walrus	lopë deti (f)	[lópə déti]
fur seal	fokë (f)	[fókə]
dolphin	delfin (m)	[dɛlfín]

bear	ari (m)	[arí]
polar bear	ari polar (m)	[arí polár]
panda	panda (f)	[pánda]

monkey	majmun (m)	[majmún]
chimpanzee	shimpanze (f)	[ʃimpánzɛ]
orangutan	orangutan (m)	[oraŋután]
gorilla	gorillë (f)	[goríɬə]
macaque	majmun makao (m)	[majmún makáo]
gibbon	gibon (m)	[gibón]

elephant	elefant (m)	[ɛlɛfánt]
rhinoceros	rinoqeront (m)	[rinocɛrónt]
giraffe	gjirafë (f)	[ɟiráfə]
hippopotamus	hipopotam (m)	[hipopotám]

| kangaroo | kangur (m) | [kaŋúr] |
| koala (bear) | koala (f) | [koála] |

mongoose	mangustë (f)	[maŋústə]
chinchilla	çinçila (f)	[tʃintʃíla]
skunk	qelbës (m)	[célbəs]
porcupine	ferrëgjatë (m)	[fɛrəɟátə]

89. Domestic animals

cat	mace (f)	[mátsɛ]
tomcat	maçok (m)	[matʃók]
dog	qen (m)	[cɛn]

horse	**kali** (m)	[káli]
stallion (male horse)	**hamshor** (m)	[hamʃór]
mare	**pelë** (f)	[pélə]

cow	**lopë** (f)	[lópə]
bull	**dem** (m)	[dém]
ox	**ka** (m)	[ka]

sheep (ewe)	**dele** (f)	[délɛ]
ram	**dash** (m)	[daʃ]
goat	**dhi** (f)	[ði]
billy goat, he-goat	**cjap** (m)	[tsjáp]

donkey	**gomar** (m)	[gomár]
mule	**mushkë** (f)	[múʃkə]

pig	**derr** (m)	[dɛr]
piglet	**derrkuc** (m)	[dɛrkúts]
rabbit	**lepur** (m)	[lépur]

hen (chicken)	**pulë** (f)	[púlə]
cock	**gjel** (m)	[ɟél]

duck	**rosë** (f)	[rósə]
drake	**rosak** (m)	[rosák]
goose	**patë** (f)	[pátə]

tom turkey, gobbler	**gjel deti i egër** (m)	[ɟél déti i égər]
turkey (hen)	**gjel deti** (m)	[ɟél déti]

domestic animals	**kafshë shtëpiake** (f)	[káfʃə ʃtəpiákɛ]
tame (e.g. ~ hamster)	**i zbutur**	[i zbútur]
to tame (vt)	**zbus**	[zbus]
to breed (vt)	**rrit**	[rit]

farm	**fermë** (f)	[férmə]
poultry	**pulari** (f)	[pularí]
cattle	**bagëti** (f)	[bagətí]
herd (cattle)	**kope** (f)	[kopé]

stable	**stallë** (f)	[stáłə]
pigsty	**stallë e derrave** (f)	[stáłə ɛ déravɛ]
cowshed	**stallë e lopëve** (f)	[stáłə ɛ lópəvɛ]
rabbit hutch	**kolibe lepujsh** (f)	[kolíbɛ lépujʃ]
hen house	**kotec** (m)	[kotéts]

90. Birds

bird	**zog** (m)	[zog]
pigeon	**pëllumb** (m)	[pəłúmb]
sparrow	**harabel** (m)	[harabél]
tit (great tit)	**xhixhimës** (m)	[dʒidʒimés]
magpie	**laraskë** (f)	[laráskə]
raven	**korb** (m)	[korb]

crow	sorrë (f)	[sórə]
jackdaw	galë (f)	[gálə]
rook	sorrë (f)	[sórə]

duck	rosë (f)	[rósə]
goose	patë (f)	[pátə]
pheasant	fazan (m)	[fazán]

eagle	shqiponjë (f)	[ʃcipóɲə]
hawk	gjeraqinë (f)	[ɟɛracínə]
falcon	fajkua (f)	[fajkúa]
vulture	hutë (f)	[hútə]
condor (Andean ~)	kondor (m)	[kondór]

swan	mjellmë (f)	[mjéɫmə]
crane	lejlek (m)	[lɛjlék]
stork	lejlek (m)	[lɛjlék]

parrot	papagall (m)	[papagáɫ]
hummingbird	kolibri (m)	[kolíbri]
peacock	pallua (m)	[paɫúa]

ostrich	struc (m)	[struts]
heron	çafkë (f)	[tʃáfkə]
flamingo	flamingo (m)	[flamíŋo]
pelican	pelikan (m)	[pɛlikán]

| nightingale | bilbil (m) | [bilbíl] |
| swallow | dallëndyshe (f) | [daɫəndýʃɛ] |

thrush	mëllenjë (f)	[mətéɲə]
song thrush	grifsha (f)	[grífʃa]
blackbird	mëllenjë (f)	[mətéɲə]

swift	dallëndyshe (f)	[daɫəndýʃɛ]
lark	thëllëzë (f)	[θəɫézə]
quail	trumcak (m)	[trumtsák]

woodpecker	qukapik (m)	[cukapík]
cuckoo	kukuvajkë (f)	[kukuvájkə]
owl	buf (m)	[buf]
eagle owl	buf mbretëror (m)	[buf mbrɛtərór]
wood grouse	fazan i pyllit (m)	[fazán i pýɫit]
black grouse	fazan i zi (m)	[fazán i zí]
partridge	thëllëzë (f)	[θəɫézə]

starling	gargull (m)	[gárguɫ]
canary	kanarinë (f)	[kanarínə]
hazel grouse	fazan mali (m)	[fazán máli]

| chaffinch | trishtil (m) | [triʃtíl] |
| bullfinch | trishtil dimri (m) | [triʃtíl dímri] |

seagull	pulëbardhë (f)	[puləbárðə]
albatross	albatros (m)	[albatrós]
penguin	penguin (m)	[pɛŋuín]

91. Fish. Marine animals

bream	krapuliq (m)	[krapulíc]
carp	krap (m)	[krap]
perch	perç (m)	[pɛrtʃ]
catfish	mustak (m)	[musták]
pike	mlysh (m)	[mlýʃ]

| salmon | salmon (m) | [salmón] |
| sturgeon | bli (m) | [blí] |

herring	harengë (f)	[haréŋə]
Atlantic salmon	salmon Atlantiku (m)	[salmón atlantíku]
mackerel	skumbri (m)	[skúmbri]
flatfish	shojzë (f)	[ʃójzə]

zander, pike perch	troftë (f)	[tróftə]
cod	merluc (m)	[mɛrlúts]
tuna	tunë (f)	[túnə]
trout	troftë (f)	[tróftə]

eel	ngjalë (f)	[ŋʲálə]
electric ray	peshk elektrik (m)	[pɛʃk ɛlɛktrík]
moray eel	ngjalë morel (f)	[ŋʲálə morél]
piranha	piranja (f)	[piráɲa]

shark	peshkaqen (m)	[pɛʃkacén]
dolphin	delfin (m)	[dɛlfín]
whale	balenë (f)	[balénə]

crab	gaforre (f)	[gafórɛ]
jellyfish	kandil deti (m)	[kandíl déti]
octopus	oktapod (m)	[oktapód]

starfish	yll deti (m)	[yɫ déti]
sea urchin	iriq deti (m)	[iríc déti]
seahorse	kalë deti (m)	[kálə déti]

oyster	midhje (f)	[míðjɛ]
prawn	karkalec (m)	[karkaléts]
lobster	karavidhe (f)	[karavíðɛ]
spiny lobster	karavidhe (f)	[karavíðɛ]

92. Amphibians. Reptiles

| snake | gjarpër (m) | [ʝárpər] |
| venomous (snake) | helmues | [hɛlmúɛs] |

viper	nepërka (f)	[nɛpérka]
cobra	kobra (f)	[kóbra]
python	piton (m)	[pitón]
boa	boa (f)	[bóa]
grass snake	kular (m)	[kulár]

| rattle snake | gjarpër me zile (m) | [ɟárpər mɛ zílɛ] |
| anaconda | anakonda (f) | [anakónda] |

lizard	hardhucë (f)	[harðútsə]
iguana	iguana (f)	[iguána]
monitor lizard	varan (m)	[varán]
salamander	salamandër (f)	[salamándər]
chameleon	kameleon (m)	[kamɛlɛón]
scorpion	akrep (m)	[akrép]

turtle	breshkë (f)	[bréʃkə]
frog	bretkosë (f)	[brɛtkósə]
toad	zhabë (f)	[ʒábə]
crocodile	krokodil (m)	[krokodíl]

93. Insects

insect	insekt (m)	[insékt]
butterfly	flutur (f)	[flútur]
ant	milingonë (f)	[miliŋónə]
fly	mizë (f)	[mízə]
mosquito	mushkonjë (f)	[muʃkóɲə]
beetle	brumbull (m)	[brúmbuɫ]

wasp	grerëz (f)	[grérəz]
bee	bletë (f)	[blétə]
bumblebee	greth (m)	[grɛθ]
gadfly (botfly)	zekth (m)	[zɛkθ]

| spider | merimangë (f) | [mɛrimáŋə] |
| spider's web | rrjetë merimange (f) | [rjétə mɛrimáɲɛ] |

dragonfly	pilivesë (f)	[pilivésə]
grasshopper	karkalec (m)	[karkaléts]
moth (night butterfly)	molë (f)	[mólə]

cockroach	kacabu (f)	[katsabú]
tick	rriqër (m)	[ríkər]
flea	plesht (m)	[plɛʃt]
midge	mushicë (f)	[muʃítsə]

locust	gjinkallë (f)	[ɟinkáɫə]
snail	kërmill (m)	[kərmíɫ]
cricket	bulkth (m)	[búlkθ]
firefly	xixëllonjë (f)	[dzidzəɫóɲə]
ladybird	mollëkuqe (f)	[moɫəkúcɛ]
cockchafer	vizhë (f)	[víʒə]

leech	shushunjë (f)	[ʃuʃúɲə]
caterpillar	vemje (f)	[vémjɛ]
earthworm	krimb toke (m)	[krímb tókɛ]
larva	larvë (f)	[lárvə]

FLORA

tree	pemë (f)	[pémə]
deciduous (adj)	gjethor	[ɟɛθór]
coniferous (adj)	halor	[halór]
evergreen (adj)	përherë të gjelbra	[pərhérə tə ɟélbra]

apple tree	pemë molle (f)	[pémə móɫɛ]
pear tree	pemë dardhe (f)	[pémə dárðɛ]
sweet cherry tree	pemë qershie (f)	[pémə cɛrʃíɛ]
sour cherry tree	pemë qershi vishnje (f)	[pémə cɛrʃí víʃɲɛ]
plum tree	pemë kumbulle (f)	[pémə kúmbuɫɛ]

birch	mështekna (f)	[məʃtékna]
oak	lis (m)	[lis]
linden tree	bli (m)	[blí]
aspen	plep i egër (m)	[plɛp i égər]
maple	panjë (f)	[páɲə]
spruce	bredh (m)	[brɛð]
pine	pishë (f)	[píʃə]
larch	larsh (m)	[lárʃ]
fir tree	bredh i bardhë (m)	[brɛð i bárðə]
cedar	kedër (m)	[kédər]

poplar	plep (m)	[plɛp]
rowan	vadhë (f)	[váðə]
willow	shelg (m)	[ʃɛlg]
alder	verr (m)	[vɛr]
beech	ah (m)	[ah]
elm	elm (m)	[élm]
ash (tree)	shelg (m)	[ʃɛlg]
chestnut	gështenjë (f)	[gəʃtéɲə]

magnolia	manjolia (f)	[maɲólia]
palm tree	palma (f)	[pálma]
cypress	qiparis (m)	[ciparís]

mangrove	rizoforë (f)	[rizofórə]
baobab	baobab (m)	[baobáb]
eucalyptus	eukalipt (m)	[ɛukalípt]
sequoia	sekuojë (f)	[sɛkuójə]

| bush | shkurre (f) | [ʃkúrɛ] |
| shrub | kaçube (f) | [katʃúbɛ] |

| grapevine | hardhi (f) | [harðí] |
| vineyard | vreshtë (f) | [vréʃtə] |

raspberry bush	mjedër (f)	[mjédər]
blackcurrant bush	kaliboba e zezë (f)	[kalibóba ɛ zézə]
redcurrant bush	kaliboba e kuqe (f)	[kalibóba ɛ kúcɛ]
gooseberry bush	shkurre kulumbrie (f)	[ʃkúrɛ kulumbríɛ]

acacia	akacie (f)	[akátsiɛ]
barberry	krespinë (f)	[krɛspínə]
jasmine	jasemin (m)	[jasɛmín]

juniper	dëllinjë (f)	[dətíɲə]
rosebush	trëndafil (m)	[trəndafíl]
dog rose	trëndafil i egër (m)	[trəndafíl i égər]

96. Fruits. Berries

| fruit | frut (m) | [frut] |
| fruits | fruta (pl) | [frúta] |

apple	mollë (f)	[móɫə]
pear	dardhë (f)	[dárðə]
plum	kumbull (f)	[kúmbuɫ]

strawberry (garden ~)	luleshtrydhe (f)	[lulɛʃtrýðɛ]
sour cherry	qershi vishnje (f)	[cɛrʃí víʃɲɛ]
sweet cherry	qershi (f)	[cɛrʃí]
grape	rrush (m)	[ruʃ]

raspberry	mjedër (f)	[mjédər]
blackcurrant	kaliboba e zezë (f)	[kalibóba ɛ zézə]
redcurrant	kaliboba e kuqe (f)	[kalibóba ɛ kúcɛ]
gooseberry	kulumbri (f)	[kulumbrí]
cranberry	boronica (f)	[boronítsa]

orange	portokall (m)	[portokáɫ]
tangerine	mandarinë (f)	[mandarínə]
pineapple	ananas (m)	[ananás]
banana	banane (f)	[banánɛ]
date	hurmë (f)	[húrmə]

lemon	limon (m)	[limón]
apricot	kajsi (f)	[kajsí]
peach	pjeshkë (f)	[pjéʃkə]

| kiwi | kivi (m) | [kívi] |
| grapefruit | grejpfrut (m) | [grɛjpfrút] |

berry	manë (f)	[mánə]
berries	mana (f)	[mána]
cowberry	boronicë mirtile (f)	[boronítsə mirtílɛ]
wild strawberry	luleshtrydhe e egër (f)	[lulɛʃtrýðɛ ɛ égər]
bilberry	boronicë (f)	[boronítsə]

97. Flowers. Plants

flower	lule (f)	[lúlɛ]
bouquet (of flowers)	buqetë (f)	[bucétə]
rose (flower)	trëndafil (m)	[trəndafíl]
tulip	tulipan (m)	[tulipán]
carnation	karafil (m)	[karafíl]
gladiolus	gladiolë (f)	[gladiólə]
cornflower	lule misri (f)	[lúlɛ mísri]
harebell	lule këmborë (f)	[lúlɛ kəmbórə]
dandelion	luleradhiqe (f)	[lulɛraðícɛ]
camomile	kamomil (m)	[kamomíl]
aloe	aloe (f)	[alóɛ]
cactus	kaktus (m)	[kaktús]
rubber plant, ficus	fikus (m)	[fíkus]
lily	zambak (m)	[zambák]
geranium	barbarozë (f)	[barbarózə]
hyacinth	zymbyl (m)	[zymbýl]
mimosa	mimoza (f)	[mimóza]
narcissus	narcis (m)	[nartsís]
nasturtium	lule këmbore (f)	[lúlɛ kəmbórɛ]
orchid	orkide (f)	[orkidé]
peony	bozhure (f)	[boʒúrɛ]
violet	vjollcë (f)	[vjóɫtsə]
pansy	lule vjollca (f)	[lúlɛ vjóɫtsa]
forget-me-not	mosmëharro (f)	[mosməharó]
daisy	margaritë (f)	[margarítə]
poppy	lulëkuqe (f)	[luləkúcɛ]
hemp	kërp (m)	[kérp]
mint	mendër (f)	[méndər]
lily of the valley	zambak i fushës (m)	[zambák i fúʃəs]
snowdrop	luleborë (f)	[lulɛbórə]
nettle	hithra (f)	[híθra]
sorrel	lëpjeta (f)	[ləpjéta]
water lily	zambak uji (m)	[zambák úji]
fern	fier (m)	[fíɛr]
lichen	likene (f)	[likénɛ]
conservatory (greenhouse)	serrë (f)	[sérə]
lawn	lëndinë (f)	[ləndínə]
flowerbed	kënd lulishteje (m)	[kənd lulíʃtɛjɛ]
plant	bimë (f)	[bímə]
grass	bar (m)	[bar]
blade of grass	fije bari (f)	[fíjɛ bári]

leaf	gjeth (m)	[ɟɛθ]
petal	petale (f)	[pɛtálɛ]
stem	bisht (m)	[biʃt]
tuber	zhardhok (m)	[ʒarðók]

| young plant (shoot) | filiz (m) | [filíz] |
| thorn | gjemb (m) | [ɟémb] |

to blossom (vi)	lulëzoj	[luləzój]
to fade, to wither	vyshket	[výʃkɛt]
smell (odour)	aromë (f)	[arómə]
to cut (flowers)	pres lulet	[prɛs lúlɛt]
to pick (a flower)	mbledh lule	[mbléð lúlɛ]

98. Cereals, grains

grain	drithë (m)	[dríθə]
cereal crops	drithëra (pl)	[dríθəra]
ear (of barley, etc.)	kaush (m)	[kaúʃ]

wheat	grurë (f)	[grúrə]
rye	thekër (f)	[θékər]
oats	tërshërë (f)	[tərʃérə]
millet	mel (m)	[mɛl]
barley	elb (m)	[ɛlb]

maize	misër (m)	[mísər]
rice	oriz (m)	[oríz]
buckwheat	hikërr (m)	[híkər]

pea plant	bizele (f)	[bizélɛ]
kidney bean	groshë (f)	[gróʃə]
soya	sojë (f)	[sójə]
lentil	thjerrëz (f)	[θjérəz]
beans (pulse crops)	fasule (f)	[fasúlɛ]

COUNTRIES OF THE WORLD

99. Countries. Part 1

Afghanistan	**Afganistan** (m)	[afganistán]
Albania	**Shqipëri** (f)	[ʃcipərí]
Argentina	**Argjentinë** (f)	[arɟɛntínə]
Armenia	**Armeni** (f)	[armɛní]
Australia	**Australia** (f)	[australía]
Austria	**Austri** (f)	[austrí]
Azerbaijan	**Azerbajxhan** (m)	[azɛrbajdʒán]
The Bahamas	**Bahamas** (m)	[bahámas]
Bangladesh	**Bangladesh** (m)	[baŋladéʃ]
Belarus	**Bjellorusi** (f)	[bjɛɫorusí]
Belgium	**Belgjikë** (f)	[bɛʎíkə]
Bolivia	**Bolivi** (f)	[boliví]
Bosnia and Herzegovina	**Bosnje Herzegovina** (f)	[bósɲɛ hɛrzɛgovína]
Brazil	**Brazil** (m)	[brazíl]
Bulgaria	**Bullgari** (f)	[buɫgarí]
Cambodia	**Kamboxhia** (f)	[kambódʒia]
Canada	**Kanada** (f)	[kanadá]
Chile	**Kili** (m)	[kíli]
China	**Kinë** (f)	[kínə]
Colombia	**Kolumbi** (f)	[kolumbí]
Croatia	**Kroaci** (f)	[kroatsí]
Cuba	**Kuba** (f)	[kúba]
Cyprus	**Qipro** (f)	[cípro]
Czech Republic	**Republika Çeke** (f)	[rɛpublíka tʃékɛ]
Denmark	**Danimarkë** (f)	[danimárkə]
Dominican Republic	**Republika Dominikane** (f)	[rɛpublíka dominikánɛ]
Ecuador	**Ekuador** (m)	[ɛkuadór]
Egypt	**Egjipt** (m)	[ɛɟípt]
England	**Angli** (f)	[aŋlí]
Estonia	**Estoni** (f)	[ɛstoní]
Finland	**Finlandë** (f)	[finlándə]
France	**Francë** (f)	[frántsə]
French Polynesia	**Polinezia Franceze** (f)	[polinɛzía frantsézɛ]
Georgia	**Gjeorgji** (f)	[ɟɛorɟí]
Germany	**Gjermani** (f)	[ɟermaní]
Ghana	**Gana** (f)	[gána]
Great Britain	**Britani e Madhe** (f)	[brítani ɛ máðɛ]
Greece	**Greqi** (f)	[grɛcí]
Haiti	**Haiti** (m)	[haíti]
Hungary	**Hungari** (f)	[huŋarí]

100. Countries. Part 2

Iceland	Islandë (f)	[islándə]
India	Indi (f)	[indí]
Indonesia	Indonezi (f)	[indonɛzí]
Iran	Iran (m)	[irán]
Iraq	Irak (m)	[irak]
Ireland	Irlandë (f)	[irlándə]
Israel	Izrael (m)	[izraél]
Italy	Itali (f)	[italí]

Jamaica	Xhamajka (f)	[dʒamájka]
Japan	Japoni (f)	[japoní]
Jordan	Jordani (f)	[jordaní]
Kazakhstan	Kazakistan (m)	[kazakistán]
Kenya	Kenia (f)	[kénia]
Kirghizia	Kirgistan (m)	[kirgistán]
Kuwait	Kuvajt (m)	[kuvájt]

Laos	Laos (m)	[láos]
Latvia	Letoni (f)	[lɛtoní]
Lebanon	Liban (m)	[libán]
Libya	Libia (f)	[libía]
Liechtenstein	Lichtenstein (m)	[litshtɛnstéin]
Lithuania	Lituani (f)	[lituaní]
Luxembourg	Luksemburg (m)	[luksɛmbúrg]

North Macedonia	Maqedonia (f)	[macɛdonía]
Madagascar	Madagaskar (m)	[madagaskár]
Malaysia	Malajzi (f)	[malajzí]
Malta	Maltë (f)	[máltə]
Mexico	Meksikë (f)	[mɛksíkə]

Moldova, Moldavia	Moldavi (f)	[moldaví]
Monaco	Monako (f)	[monáko]
Mongolia	Mongoli (f)	[moŋolí]
Montenegro	Mali i Zi (m)	[máli i zí]
Morocco	Marok (m)	[marók]
Myanmar	Mianmar (m)	[mianmár]

Namibia	Namibia (f)	[namíbia]
Nepal	Nepal (m)	[nɛpál]
Netherlands	Holandë (f)	[holándə]
New Zealand	Zelandë e Re (f)	[zɛlándə ɛ ré]
North Korea	Korea e Veriut (f)	[koréa ɛ vériut]
Norway	Norvegji (f)	[norvɛɟí]

101. Countries. Part 3

Pakistan	Pakistan (m)	[pakistán]
Palestine	Palestinë (f)	[palɛstínə]
Panama	Panama (f)	[panamá]
Paraguay	Paraguai (m)	[paraguái]

Peru	Peru (f)	[pɛrú]
Poland	Poloni (f)	[poloní]
Portugal	Portugali (f)	[portugalí]
Romania	Rumani (f)	[rumaní]
Russia	Rusi (f)	[rusí]

Saudi Arabia	Arabia Saudite (f)	[arabía saudítɛ]
Scotland	Skoci (f)	[skotsí]
Senegal	Senegal (m)	[sɛnɛgál]
Serbia	Serbi (f)	[sɛrbí]
Slovakia	Sllovaki (f)	[sɬovakí]
Slovenia	Sllovenia (f)	[sɬovɛnía]

South Africa	Afrika e Jugut (f)	[afríka ɛ júgut]
South Korea	Korea e Jugut (f)	[koréa ɛ júgut]
Spain	Spanjë (f)	[spáɲə]
Suriname	Surinam (m)	[surinám]
Sweden	Suedi (f)	[suɛdí]
Switzerland	Zvicër (f)	[zvítsər]
Syria	Siri (f)	[sirí]

Taiwan	Tajvan (m)	[tajván]
Tajikistan	Taxhikistan (m)	[tadʒikistán]
Tanzania	Tanzani (f)	[tanzaní]
Tasmania	Tasmani (f)	[tasmaní]
Thailand	Tajlandë (f)	[tajlándə]
Tunisia	Tunizi (f)	[tunizí]
Turkey	Turqi (f)	[turcí]
Turkmenistan	Turkmenistan (m)	[turkmɛnistán]

Ukraine	Ukrainë (f)	[ukraínə]
United Arab Emirates	Emiratet e Bashkuara Arabe (pl)	[ɛmirátɛt ɛ baʃkúara árábɛ]
United States of America	Shtetet e Bashkuara të Amerikës	[ʃtétɛt ɛ baʃkúara tə amɛríkəs]
Uruguay	Uruguai (m)	[uruguái]
Uzbekistan	Uzbekistan (m)	[uzbɛkistán]

Vatican City	Vatikan (m)	[vatikán]
Venezuela	Venezuelë (f)	[vɛnɛzuélə]
Vietnam	Vietnam (m)	[viɛtnám]
Zanzibar	Zanzibar (m)	[zanzibár]